LUKE BENOIT

ALL STORMS PASS

THE ANTI-MEDITATIONS

ISBN: 0615520138
ISBN-13: 9780615520131

Createspace, Charleston, South Carolina

*for my Mom, Dad and Auntie Cia who
deserved a book a long time ago.*

ALL STORMS PASS

THE ANTI-MEDITATIONS

AYANA —
I can tell
you are so fun.
We are going
to have a
BLAST !

Mark

The Statement of High Self-Esteem:

1. Every person deserves the right to live with HIGH SELF-ESTEEM.

2. If anyone ever told you that you were anything less than wonderful… they lied. The problem now is that at some time in the past you swallowed and believed their lies and you are still living them out in the form of your current problems.

Today I will admit that
in order to deal with my Anger
I must admit that I have sadness
or grief underneath that
I must allow myself to

feel.

Today I will remember that:

I AM A SURVIVOR.

I have been through a lot,
I am still here and
It is not over for me yet

and I am stronger than I know
and

this is a decision I must make

Today I will remember the rule that:

What I resist persists.

Whenever I am kicking and screaming
or fighting against something,
I am usually digging myself in more stuck
and causing myself more pain.

(Almost always, the answer is to
 Let Go)

Sometimes there is a reason that the road
isn't unfolding in front of me just yet...
even if I can't see what that reason is now.

It is true that the world and its people are
often quite wrong
but the only person I have any power over
changing is me.

Today I will let my own
PEACE begin with me.

Today I will accept that:

Right now, there is no problem.
(in this moment,
in this very instant)

and, right now,

I am safe.

(the only problem I have is my fearful thinking
which is convincing me that I have a big problem
and I am not safe)

Today I will focus only on the next thing in front of me and the next right action and let the results take care of themselves

What would you do if you weren't afraid?

Sometimes
I am afraid
to hope

Today I will give myself permission to feel whatever it is I need to feel…

and for as long as I need to feel it.

No one can take away my feelings or make me wrong about

what I feel.

Today I will

Let go of and
Keep my Hands off
what I am trying to fix
and instead,

 Trust.

There are some things
 I will just never be able
to do anything about.

(this is beautiful because my life will become more
peaceful and happy when I can learn to accept this)

Today I will accept that there
will never be a Perfect Day

with no problems.

So I will juice out every bit
of happiness that I can find
around me today

instead of letting my life pass me

 by.

"Life is Difficult." M. Scott Peck
The Road Less Traveled

Today, I will understand and accept that

Feelings are not facts

although I feel hurt and angry
at the same time
I am still OK

Today I will let go of my
ridiculous unconscious belief
that I can predict what's going to happen
or know what should happen
in the future.

*"the moment that I let go of it
was the moment I got more than
I could handle…"* Alanis Morrisette

Support

Today I will admit that I cannot make it alone.

To get to a place where I can be healthy,
feel good about myself and have a life
that works,

I must ask for help.

This can be difficult if I have been hurt
in the past, especially by people who were
or are important to me.

I may have to learn how to trust again.

But there are safe people in the world
who can be there for me and I can find them
(even if that takes help too).

And if I don't reach out, I will probably
continue living in pain and it will be
much harder or impossible for things to

change.

Surrender

———

Ma'am, just put the gun down…

She heard what he said
 And she looked around herself
  And she knew It was true

She was out of options

She bent down and she laid
The gun on the ground
She stepped back and
She sat down

She felt it all that energy
drain out of her
there was a relief
there was a sadness
It was over
And she knew she was going to cry
But she could

 Breathe….

A long long time ago, Janis Joplin sang the words:

**Freedom's just another word for
nothing left to lose...**

I can make these words painful or beautiful.

I have a choice about how I see my life
and the world and what is handed to me.
And what I am going to do with it.

I can see loss as a reason to lay down
and give up or I can be willing
to see things differently.

I must **DECIDE** that this is my chance to
begin again and to build a life that will be
better than it ever was

before.

Today I will realize:

"The problem is not really the problem."

The fear of feeling the pain that
I have attached to the problem

(the hurt, anger, fear or even panic)

is the real problem.

If I can allow myself to feel the feelings
and learn how to surf them,
I can get through almost anything

for I am so much stronger than I know.

In spite of however I may have gotten off track
or whatever problems I may be dealing with
right now,

On the deepest level,

I am not defective
I am not broken
   and
there is nothing wrong
   with my Soul.

Today I will

"Play the tape all the way through..."

I will not think and scheme
until my brain hurts.

I will remember that I have an
Intuition that can guide me.

I will strive to practice balance in Thinking.

Today,

I will check the cheap drama
at the door

and **I will get honest with myself**
about what is really going on with me
and my problems.

I will take responsibility
for <u>only</u> my role
in what has gone wrong

and I will drop as much of the blame as
I can so that I can be free
to make new choices
and take healthy action
to move forward

Today I will notice,
take in
and anchor deep inside me
the many miracles
and occasions of beauty
that are all around me

(instead of missing out because I am absorbed only in my
immediate troubles)

Today I will notice
every negative word I say
 and even
every negative thought that
passes through my mind

And I will ask myself

"What is the benefit I am getting
 from these?"

Today I will try to understand
what SHAME really is

I will try to recognize that I am carrying it
and I will admit that it hurts.

I will understand that I can allow myself to feel it
so that I can be rid of it.

I will understand that it doesn't belong to me
and that it never belonged to me

And that I can learn how to stop carrying it
and believing that it is

   true

Today I will begin to learn to shift my perceptions
in order to heal my depression and grief, anger and fear and panic.

"Nervous breakdowns can be a highly underrated method of spiritual transformation….As painful as that experience was, I now see it as an important, perhaps necessary step in my breakthrough to a happier life."

---Marianne Williamson,
A Return to Love

Today I will:

Mind
My
Own
Business

I will stay out of anyone else's head:

Whatever my fears are
I can't have any idea about
what you might be thinking
and I have no control over your

decisions

*"…I feel like I got shot, I just didn't fall down…
and I got a big chain around my neck
and I'm broken down like a train wreck
well, it's over and I know it
but I can't let go…"* ----Lucinda Williams

they say that pain comes standard in
every life but suffering is optional

How I talk to my self (my self-talk) is crucial
to how I experience my life.
I have a choice to create drama or
to comfort myself many many times each day

Making this decision is a skill I must learn
and consciously practice.

Even Chicken Little learned that
the sky wasn't really falling

There is an energy
that is making the world turn
and the wind move in the trees
and my heart beat
and a baby grow in his
     Mama's belly

THERE IS NOTHING WRONG
WITH ME

I AM JUST FINE
THE WAY I AM

Today, I will accept you
Exactly as you are.

I will stop wishing
you would change,

not so that I can forgive you
but so that I can have peace

People do not change.
Unless they really want to
And they do hard work
Over a period of time
And they use tools
And they get help.

Today I will become aware of
the many ways I use
to escape unpleasant reality.

I will practice noticing when I am doing this
and ask myself what may be
going on

underneath.

I make assumptions and

I have expectations.

Today, I will become aware
of how I fill in the

blanks

Today I will try not to take
anything Personally for 24 hours

Maybe, just
maybe….

they're not doing it **to** me.

maybe they're just doing it...?

Today I will be aware of the unspoken

"RULES OF THE DYSFUNCTIONAL FAMILY"

Don't see it
Don't hear it
Don't feel it –and-
Don't tell it.

I will look inside of me to see
which of these rules
I am still carrying

And I will no longer
let them lead to my own

Self-destruction.

Transcendence

Giving up can be a point of defeat or a point of starting over.

I have a choice to make this a story about suffering and dying or more about the rising again.

*"When you got nuthin,
You got nuthin' left to
lose…"*
                                    -Bob Dylan

Today I will

decide to be on my own side

and I will learn to respect,
honor and even
Love myself.

And if anyone thinks this is conceited
or slings me any crap about this,
I will **ignore** them.
I will let them keep their judgment, fear and
ignorance.

And I will accept that this Truth is
what the Universe wants for me
and for everyone.

And I will realize that my denial of this
is one of the primary sources of my

problems.

'There is no greater agony
than bearing
an untold story
inside you.'
~ Maya Angelou

Today I will realize and accept
that I need to find people
in this world I can trust,
that I can and
that I cannot get better
and live healthy all alone.

Today I will decide:

I like me.

I won't be ashamed of it.
And if you think I'm conceited
or you don't like me because of it –

Too bad for you.

Because if you don't like me
and you are judging me
for whatever reason,
chances are, you probably
don't like yourself

Trust the Flow
(it's going happen anyway.
Fighting it will only knot you up inside)

Clean house
(get your side of the street clean
so that you can let go of the guilt
and any garbage you may be carrying)

Help others
(but never to the detriment of your own health.
If you don't put you first,
you will have nothing left to give to anybody else)

*When I take personal responsibility
I become free.*

today I will let go of
trying to **GET**
from you what I want

instead I will focus on
giving you what
I would like to receive
and treating you the way
I would like be treated

(honor, respect, acceptance, forgiveness,
approval, unconditional positive regard…)

I need to learn how to not get my way

(in the long run, it won't work for me)

When I push people to do what I want
when they don't really want to
they may go along with it

but they will resent it
and they will hold onto it
and in the end,

it will push them away

Obsession

is another word for pain killer or
distraction….

I want to be in control
because I think we are not safe
even though I do not walk around
Saying to myself
"I am not safe…"

Most of the time we distract ourselves
so that we won't even be aware
of our fear or have to feel it.

Today I will let myself be aware
of my fears so that
I can see through them

(drugs, sex, rock and roll, physical illness, depression,
helping, worrying, working, bla-bla….)

Longing for someone
is not Love

Longing for someone
is not Being Loved

Just be.

(no try, no win, no get, "*Imagine there's no Heaven*")

Today,

I will live in reality

Not a "Wish" projection reality of what
I hope my life will be
or a "Doomsday" dread story
of all the bad things that will happen.

And I will take the actions of living
that are appropriate and in line with
my best/clearest understanding
 of what the Truth
of my current life situation

is

Today,

For 24 hours

I will not

sneak,

manipulate

or lie

even when I think it is for a good cause.

I will live in integrity.

If I expect difficult situations to go
perfectly
I am setting myself up for
disappointment and pain.

I will accept that bumps in the road are
part of life
and understand that just because my
problem
is not solved right away does not
mean
that I am being punished.

imperfection is perfection
LIFE IS NOT A STRAIGHT LINE

Today, I will learn not to be

> Your excuse
> Your distraction
> Your scapegoat
> or Your supposed "Problem"

anymore.

I will realize that I need to release the garbage that anybody has put on me in the past and find out who "**I**" am.

When they pulled the curtain back
everybody finally saw that the great
big Giant Head was nothing but smoke
and mirrors and that all there was

behind there

was a scared and pathetic little old man.

Sometimes one fear may Masquerade as another

And sometimes what is
Worse than the fact that you've
Left me is my
Leaving myself

In order to get better,
I must face my deeper fears
About myself
And the world
And not just losing a drug
Or a person
Or a wish I had that I was using
To distract me from my deepest pain

Sometimes one fear may masquerade as another

in order to get better
I will need to see underneath
the fears I immediately see
to the deeper fears
they are

hiding

Today, I will take care of
business
and I will put First things First

I will realize that this day, this week,
this moment
are only temporary

I will stop searching for
<u>the</u> missing piece that will
fix everything and realize
there is no such thing.

And if there were
there would be many many more
than just one.

If I don't show you who I really am
then you can't really love me

If I don't learn to be
completely open and available
to myself,

I can't say that I really love you:

**Today I will become aware
of the MASKS
I present to myself
and to the world**

For both of us
I will find out
who I really am

today, I will say "NO"

when I mean to
when I want to
and when I need to

I will not just avoid you
and keep my mouth shut
to avoid conflict or feeling uncomfortable
or to please you

or even just to get a little revenge

(I will take responsibility for using
silence as a weapon or for control)

I will not **work** you and be passive-aggressive
or expect you to *psychic-ly* "know."

I will live in integrity
and have the courage to admit that
if I say "no," you might reject me
and sometimes life hurts.

This is called *intimacy.*

Today, I will not push
feelings and emotions
which I decide
are negative away

I will recognize that they are
Necessary as part
of a process of
moving me forward
But they are not necessarily

True.

I will let myself feel

**Today, I will realize that
it is possible that
some of my negative thoughts
could be not -100%- true**

For 24 hours,
when an upsetting idea comes up,
I will consider that there is a possibility
this thought *could be* untrue

and that there is a possibility
that the opposite positive
of what I'm afraid of
could be true

today I will learn to listen to

my Intuition

When I do not know how to do
or I do not see the next step,
sometimes I forget that
there is a deeper knowing available to me.

I am not restricted to my own
limited logic or understanding

I can learn to listen to the guidance of
the still quietest place inside me
my intuition, my spirit – my center…
where I know the

Truth.

(while I still may not see the whole pathway,
 my next steps become clear)

Today I will let myself feel

I will feel all of my feelings
and not push them away
including fear, anger
and sadness

so that I don't cheat myself
out of feeling the happiness.

Feeling all of my feelings
sooner or later
is a necessary part of
the process and
unless I do it

I will not get better

If there are no coincidences,
then what am I doing here

in this place
on this spot
in this instant within
this very moment
right now?

(do I have a purpose and, if so, what is it?)

<u>Sometimes I blow things out of proportion</u>

sometimes I take things personally
and it hurts more than it should
when I think that you've hurt me

and sometimes
I hurt more than I should
when you blame me
and I feel compelled
to **fix** it

There is "me"
and there is who you think I am
and there is who I think I am

and beyond this, there is
who I Really am,

the True Self I have forgotten.

Today, I will learn to tell
the difference.

An old saying goes:

"HAPPINESS IS NOT
<u>GETTING</u> WHAT YOU WANT.

HAPPINESS IS WANTING
WHAT YOU HAVE."

Today, I will learn
to want what I have
(and be satisfied)

There is a possibility that
it's OK that I don't know right now
or I can't see how
things are going to change.

more will be revealed

am I looking for the silver lining or am I driven to find the very darkest part of the cloud?

If *"all behavior is purposeful,"* (Freud)
am I willing to look at
my commitment to
my negativity and my misery?

What am I getting out of it?
What would I lose if I let it go?

And can I even be willing and honest enough
to admit that this might be the truth about me?

Today,

I will become aware of

where I put my focus

When I find myself filling with worry
or fear that seems so real and
important right now, I will stop myself
and remember:

THIS JUST

REALLY ISN'T

THAT IMPORTANT.

I will remember that there are
things in my life that really matter
and that are truly critical to my happiness

**today I will choose not to be
be in any relationship
under false pretenses**

because it can never
be in my best interest

and no matter what my
intentions are

the truth will always
come out in the wash

Today I will not wait for the "someday"

when I will not be afraid before I act.

Today, I will feel

the fear and

I will do it anyway.

----

cour·age [kur-ij]

— n

1. the power or quality of dealing with or facing danger, fear, pain, etc

2. the courage of one's convictions; the confidence to act in accordance with one's beliefs

Even the happiest, most well adjusted person goes through periods of doubt, and times when they don't want to look in the mirror.

Today, I will realize that everyone has down times and that having some lows is normal and just part of the deal.

Today I will remember the axiom:

If you spot it
you got it

How often am I willing to consider
that what I don't like about you
is also probably true about me?

Criticism, judgment, humiliation
and sarcasm are all usually
forms of fear.

1. WHEN I PUT MYSELF DOWN PEOPLE FIND IT ANNOYING.

Most people have struggles with self-esteem. Sometimes it can be hard to believe in yourself.

I need to make a decision to DECIDE to make things better.

I can ask for help.

But no one wants to join me in my misery.

2. PEOPLE WHO FEEL GOOD ABOUT THEMSELVES ARE THE ONES WHO ARE ATTRACTIVE.

WE LIKE TO BE AROUND THEM.

We often get confused about the difference between high self-esteem and conceit.

Much of our world teaches us that feeling good about ourselves is a "sin."

I need to drop the old programming.

today, just for one day

I will not try to figure EVERYTHING out

I will pick only
one or two pieces,
even then
knowing that

I might get those wrong too.

re·lax [ri-laks] – verb

1. to make less tense or rigid
2. to make less strict or severe

Today I will snap out of it.

Yes, there are things in the future that are probably inevitable.

We will all have losses.

Some people we love will die.

There will be illness.

Most people suffer pain over money, heartbreak and family problems.

But I will realize:

Welcome to the world.

I am not that special.

Today I will not let my fear about the future ruin this moment,

this day and its potential for happiness.

Today I will let myself
not care

about the one thing

that is consuming me

I will take a 24 hour vacation

It will still be there tomorrow if I need it then.

There is no

Magic Wand

Love is not adrenaline.

Love is more about work

than it is about intoxication

or candlelight or flowers

or candy and sexy times.

Today I will decide whether I am willing to let go of the idea
that any drug or illusion can come in like a magic wand
and make me and my problematic life

all **"Fine."**

Today I will try to

live in Reality

and **what is**

rather than

how I **wish** things could be

or I think they **should** be

and I will learn

to tell the difference

(and sometimes reality is better and more positive

than the "reality" I am projecting)

Today I will be honest about

whether I want to change

or whether I just want to **talk**

even when I have good intentions
if I don't take action, nothing will get different

I need to be honest with myself before I can
be honest with anyone else

*(sometimes I don't even know that I'm just
talking)*

Today I will ask myself:

Do you want to be right, or do you want to be happy?

Is it worth the price of my calm, my composure

or my piece of mind to not "let you win?"

If I do, what have I lost?

Do I have a need to make you wrong?

do I have the ability

to just let the other person

have the last word?

Today I will ask myself:

Am I nodding and smiling

and *"AGREEING"* with you

just to shut you up?

am I respecting you or me when I am doing this?

and what will be the price for both of us?

what has the price of this

been for me in the past?

sometimes I haven't "done anything to deserve this."

When I am in real pain, in my frustration, I ask:

"WHY? WHY?" and

"WHAT HAVE I DONE TO DESERVE THIS?"

as if I'm doing something wrong or there is something that I am

supposed to do be doing that

– if I could just figure out –

would let everything be fine.

sometimes **I'm not doing anything wrong** and

there's nothing I'm missing.

but the pain is part of the process of getting me to where I need to go

– although I can't see it until I'm looking back from the other side.

Today I will compliment

the people around me

honestly and sincerely only

and only when it is true

and I will notice if I

may also be treated differently

and I will notice

how I feel inside

Today, I will not fight my

Fear of Uncertainty

and get myself whipped up

Into a Frenzy

I will realize that I cannot

tell the future

I will stop chanting

"I can't take it!

I can't take it!"

and I will do my best to realize

that even though I don't know

what is going to happen

I am still OK

which I will realize from the

other side and with perspective

Today for 24 hours

I will stop to question

my **DISTRUST**

and I will ask myself

how much of what I am

experiencing now

really belongs here in the present

and how much of it is

my old programming from the past

that is being triggered

and I will try to separate out

the difference

I AM NOT MY PAST

(I am not my money

I am not my kids

I am not my marriage

I am not my job

I am not my friends

I am not my family…)

Today I will not make you responsible for my happiness.

I will not wait until someday

when you give me what I want,

or what I think you should,

what I think you owe me

or what I think I need from you.

(Today I will release you)

I will understand and accept

that some people are unable

to say "No."

There are many ways to say "NO"

without coming out and using the word.

For today, I will not set myself up

like Charlie Brown and Lucy

with the

football.

Today I will realize:

I am not just here

to get everything I can.

I am here to give

They say that this is the key to real happiness.

But no matter what has happened to me

in the past, I need to find a healthy balance.

Gratitude is an Action

not just a **Word** or a **Feeling**

Today I will look at

"who I have made grateful this year?"

If it seems good I will take it in and really feel it

If I think it wasn't enough,

I will let myself "Boo hoo hoo" about it but

minimally only for

 I cannot change the past.

Then moderately, I will get to work to

 to do what I need to do make me different

If sad or empty Let Downs come during the Holidays, I will say: "Bring it on…"

There is no "**perfect family**" or equivalent

that I may think I need to have in my own life.

Today, I will really get that all the *"bla bla bla"*

the Television and the Media and the culture

have fed me aren't realistic for most people.

I can insist that "bad" feelings I might have shouldn't be there or I can learn to get past them and ride them out.

"<u>What would I be without my story</u>?"

without the achievements and the trophies

that I think contribute to me and make

me valuable

or the baggages and guilt and ghosts.

both the positives and negatives that I think

make me who I am but actually

make me forget that I am not

limited by the past.

----

there was who I was

and there was who I was told I was

and there is who I am being told I am now

and who they tell me I will be

and there will be who and what I really will be

and then there is who I am
  (now)

  (and only one of them is real)

in between days...

(HOPE IS A DECISION)

Sometimes, you're not where you're going

yet and not even completely done with

where you've just been

Sometimes I can't wait for the future

just because I want to get the hell out of here

but my life is happening right now

and if I'm not paying attention

I just might miss it

and it might pass me by

being in between is part of the deal

And it's where the past becomes a part of
who I am

Today, can you dare to say to your to yourself

– ALL DAY

"I am wonderful"

and mean it?

Can you say it about someone else?

and if you can, what makes you so

"Special" (and arrogant) that you should

believe there is something so bad about you

that you don't deserve it too?

(the Universe does not make junk.
Why should I be the exception?)

I will let myself imagine

just the possibility that

the Universe wants me

to be Happy

(really)

and my only job is to stay out of the way

and to do my best to stop trying to control

to accept that I don't know

what the variables should be

or how they should fall together to create

that Happiness.

Today I will remember:

I am already complete.

Nothing external can add to me

or compensate for any

imagined deficits that make me feel

depressed or less than

and needing to escape from

the "reality" of my life

and who I think I am

Lasting happiness cannot come from

without or

outside me

Today I will

develop the strong Understanding

to see beyond the Present
Moment

and my immediate situation

so that I may release my

feeling like a victim

that life is out to get me

and nearly constant feelings of sadness,

hopelessness and anger

and even while I am in the middle of it

I will recognize the greater good

that will come out of the hard time

I'm going through right now.

(paraphrase from Lisa Nichols, <u>No Matter What</u>)

Today I will trust that

That I am in the right place

<u>and at the right time</u>

that we have come together

as the exactly the right people

to together create

the perfect changes

we each need

right now

(and whether I am aware of it or not this is

happening not just today but everyday)

Today I will remember that

(almost always)

when someone is angry at me

it is more about the anger

they have towards themselves

and more than for anything that's going on

between us right now

It's easier to deal with someone who is attacking you if you realize that inside they are attacking themselves.

Even if they don't see it. And we all do this.

ob·ses·sion

–noun

1. the domination of one's thoughts or feelings by a persistent idea, image, desire, etc.

2. the idea, image, desire, feeling, etc., itself.

my OBSESSIONS create a fiction I believe

that I am incomplete and I **need** something

outside of me to fix me and that something outside

can be added to me and can fix me

Today I will become aware of what my obsessions are

and what unpleasant feelings/ reality

I am using them to avoid

Today I will realize that

Sometimes I am disconnected

from my feelings

but that doesn't mean

they aren't there

———

*He said: "**Uh, I don't know.**"*

*And then she said: "**Don't you have any feelings!!??**"*

And then he didn't say anything.

They both didn't realize the feelings were there, underneath.

So many feelings that he couldn't open his mouth.

But they were just locked down so tight that it felt

– for both of them – just like they'd been removed.

Today I will realize that I have a

CHOICE about how I

INTERPRET change

and what meanings I put onto it

change can be frightening.

When the pieces on the board move,

I can't know what to expect

Anymore.

I think I am losing control but

I have forgotten –

I was never really in control

in the first place

Today

I will not predicate my

will to live

or my Happiness on any anyone else

I will allow myself to accept that that person in my life

I have been waiting for to change either

      a) may not change – or –

      b) isn't going to change (ever) and

      c) at least hasn't changed as of today.

BUT I WILL NOT PUT MY LIFE

ON HOLD ANY LONGER.

I have the choice to do what it takes

to not blame you and strand myself

in painful hopes - hanging by my fingernails.

And learning to love you exactly as you are –

(here or gone) will make me strong.

Today,

<u>I will not beg you to love me</u>

no matter who you are to me

my husband or my wife. my brother or my sister
my parent or my child. my partner or my lover
my friend, my boss. my teacher. my classmate

my enemy.

When I "Love" you with obsession and need, then I
can't see you for who YOU really are – independent
of what "I" need from you

whether its approval or sex, $, instructions, etc, etc.
etc…or even just your physical presence

because I don't want to be

alone.

I have to see YOU
beyond my needs and
—even with the purest intentions—
that is no

easy trick.

today, I will realize that

my defenses

are protecting me as much

from betrayal

as they are

from Love

and as much

from hurt

as they are

from healing

sometimes I invent ways to

push people away

without knowing it

maybe by trying to control or boss them

maybe by being too ready to attack them for

abandoning me

using me

dominating me

taking advantage of me

or putting one over on me

some other way.

sometimes I don't see it

when somebody is already on my side.

Today I will forgive you and let go of
the POISON that is **blocking** me from
moving forward and the good things
I deserve to have
in my life

Every time I make you guilty,

I am blocking myself from moving forward

(instead I want to be free)

Who have I not forgiven, released or LET GO?

and what do I believe I am guilty of

which makes me so convinced that I don't deserve?

What in me clings to blaming myself?

Today I will choose to understand that

<u>you</u> are not your mistakes

which means I am not my mistakes either

Today I will realize:

I do not need to TRY to

make anything happen.

I will not push or try to work you to get what I want.

I will remember that it didn't work last time

and even if I do get my way like this

I may lose it anyway

and push the people away who were in my way

    – like road kill.

I will realize that when I simply

let things fall into place and drop

my resistance and insistence

and just **DO** what shows up in front of me

one next indicated action at a time

I'm much more likely to get what I want.

Today I will realize:

"*I need do nothing...*"

WHAT I AM WITHHOLDING FROM YOU I AM WITHHOLDING FROM MYSELF

(can I allow myself to have it?

can I believe I deserve it?)

Today, I will stop waiting FOR ALL THE STARS TO ALIGN

Today I will give up the wish and the fantasy that someday the stars will align, that someday it will be perfect and everything will fall into place.

Because maybe this is it, right now…and the Happy Destiny is the road and not the destination and it's already here.

"Stop dreaming, anticipating. Stop reaching for that distant star. You've been waiting. Don't pass this moment. The light's before your very eyes…" (Donna Summer, *All Through the Night*)

Today I will understand

I will have the life
I believe and feel I deserve

Most of us spend our lives

trying to be an Engine struggling

trying to get what we want from the world or life

or someone else

what if the problem isn't what I'm not getting

but what I can't let in

what I'm not allowing to come to me...

what I'm not able to receive

Maybe when I believe (deeply) that I am lovable,

then I will be loved and when I believe that I deserve

to have money and happiness and good things

then I will have those too

Today,

I will enjoy the "You" that is here in front of me right now

without trying
to tie you down
to the needs
I think I have for you
in the **Future.**

Today, I will accept that
YOU DON'T OWE ME ANYTHING

"I've heard it said
that people come into our lives
for a reason bringing
something we must learn
and we are led to those who
help us most to grow
if we let them
and we help them in return..."
----from "<u>Wicked.</u>"

Sometimes people come and go
in our lives
in all sorts of contexts
It can be sweet or bitter

we have a choice
in our relationships
to choose combat

or to know that
–no matter how long it lasts –
whether I like it or not

it will be a learning experience.

Putting demands on you
will never work -
for you can never be

the **source** of my
or our happiness
(which can only come
from within).

The more prescriptions and requirements
I try to place on you
the more I will push you away
and whether we like it or not
or how easy it is to forget...

You don't owe me anything

and so I don't owe you anything

and so we are both free.

BE BLANK

The most powerful state to exist

in is one where I am totally open

without prescription and expectations,

demands of what my life <u>must</u> be,

the world around me

and the people I love

When I can be blank

all anxiety drops

and like an empty canvas

me

and my life

can be written on

with the most

beautiful colors

unknown

far more beautiful

than my limited mind

and its schemes could

ever come up with

Today, I will open myself

as completely as I can

to the infinite intelligence

and let it carry me

to my life's bursting

like a Firework in

greatest possibility

and out of my own way

Today I will notice the thoughts that are coming and going without my noticing

Including the ones that are passing

quickly through my mind

that I'm not even realizing

I am thinking

and before I open my mouth

and before I take action

I will consider consequences

and I will realize that none of

my thoughts are neutral.

Meditation for New Year's Eve:

Today,

I will not regret the past or

wish to shut the door on it.

I will only look back to enjoy

to celebrate (and rave in my truest heart)

the beauty and the good that have been

so that I may better see where I need to go now

and look for clues to how I might get there

I will not steep in a jacuzzi of my own self-pity

or misery or negativity or regret

...and I will be amazed at how I can

find a new freedom and a new happiness,

that my whole attitude and outlook on Life

can change and I can know Peace.

   (– paraphrasing from the AA Big Blue Book)

Mediation for New Year's Day:

This year,

<u>I will want me</u>

regardless of who has ever prized me

or thrown me away

I will know that I am a good person

and that I care about others

and I will choose to be

my own champion

I will not give myself

100% <u>completely</u> to anyone

and I will not depend on anyone

who can't also feel good about

themselves too

I will not carry anyone else's dead weight

or let anyone else control my life

and I will not lose myself in trying to please

Today I will ask the Universe:

please take every relationship in my life.

(because I think I know, but I don't know)

Help me to drop all of my agendas

and let go of what I want to get out of the other person.

Instead of – " Get me what I want..."

Let this relationship take whatever form you would choose

(whether it's the wife, husband, parent, friend, etc...

that I think I need – or not)

that it may serve its Highest possible purposes

and support the very Best possible Life for the other person

and their Greatest Happiness

I will know that no other person

owes me anything and that

not getting what I want from anyone else

cannot really take anything lasting and

True away from me.

Today,

I will at least TRY to catch myself

midstream
when I am **MAKING YOU WRONG**

and I will at least try to
SHUT MY MOUTH
if that is the best I can do

and I will realize that it is possible for me
to think a positive thought
instead...

*"People don't grow because they are
nagged or criticized or made to be wrong.
People grow because they are loved...
Sometimes we need to give someone
the gift of space..."*

----Marianne Williamson

Today,

I will realize that I am supposed to be

imperfect and mistaken along the way

Sometimes you can notice yourself

doing something that you don't want to be doing anymore

and sometimes I can see myself thinking thoughts

and thinking in ways and patterns that I know

are unproductive and don't work for me anymore,

in ways that are no longer True for me

and don't support who I want to be

today, If I fall short of my ideals

I will breathe and let go of my judgment of myself

Today,

I will realize that I deserve Unconditional Love especially from Myself.

even if I don't believe it, today I will act as if I do

that the world isn't against me and that I can relax

even if I have to Pretend

even if it seems like these are just words

I know that there are at least some people

I know who deserve unconditional love

and I will realize that I am **not** different from those people

that I deserve the same and that

on some level I think I am getting something out of

not giving it to myself

Today,

I will notice the "Boxcar" thoughts

– conditions, worries, demands

and contingencies –

I attach to my situations

and I will remember to remember

that the things I think I want

and the goals I have set

may not be what's

truly best

for me...

How often have I gotten what I really wanted

only to find there were complications

or that what I thought would make me happy

didn't turn out to really make me happy

or even made me feel worse because it

didn't turn out to be the solution

I'd hoped it would be

Today I will realize that I am already

perfect, whole and complete and that

there are no external things I can add to myself

to make me valuable or any better

Today,

I will give up the

"But…"

or the "YEAH, BUT…"

_____

I will realize that when I interrupt you

and don't let you finish what you're saying all the way

because *"You don't understand…"* or

I **know** that I know better

I will own that I am showing you that

You and what you have to say

DON'T MATTER to me

  (that maybe you don't even exist)

and I will stop second guessing myself

and giving myself reasons why I can't do

what I'm afraid to do

and I will realize that my trying to foretell,

outwit and pre-program the future is working

"SO WELL" for me!

sometimes

When I am hit by an

EMOTIONAL TRUCK

I can be dragged for a long long way

and I may sustain painful injuries

that leave scars

I can't see that

it's bringing me to a more beautiful place

and it's not "by accident"

where I will be wiser

and more compassionate

and I will know myself better

and like myself better because

I know who I am and

I know I am a

SURVIVOR

I have EVERYTHING.

Today,

I will resist my instinct to cringe

and get jealous

when I hear someone say

"One day at a time"

or other "sunshiny" statements

or if I see those yellow happy smiley faces

or equivalent stickers

on car windows and bumpers and

notebook covers

I will realize that these are Truth

even if I am suspect and they don't

come naturally for everyone

I will realize that its OK to be happy

even if there is fear that if you get it,

it could possibly not stay

and I will not reject myself for mistrusting

and I will believe and commit to the

Reality that **Happy is a right**

that belongs to everyone

and that

I already HAVE EVERYTHING.

Today I will decide

I will not be
punished <u>again</u>

I WILL NOT GO BACK into

a cycle of punishment

that was ended and

I will not let you punish me

and I will not punish you

(even if we're not hitting each other)

I will realize that when I am punishing you,

I am punishing myself

and I will take responsibility and **really** SEE

that your punishment is **but the symptom**

and not the cause and I will not buy into my own

rejection of myself any longer

I will outgrow my self-sabotage

and I will not let my poisonous beliefs

block me from all of the good things

that are meant for me…

good health

good money

good emotions

and all the good I can bring to others…

It has been said that the most painful state

a person can live in is the state in which

they have become unacceptable to his or her

own "self"

There is

NO SUBSTITUTE FOR LOVE

not love as in flowers and candy

so many people report a feeling

like an emptiness

or a "hole in my soul"

that nothing can fill

that is felt most in the quiet

when everything outside stops

and we try to put money into it

and sex and cars and people

and things and jobs and even education…

and all kinds of external things

a long time ago, someone wrote

"I once was lost but now I'm found"

 and often losing these kinds of things

not getting them is the beginning

of a "self-forgetting" (with a little s)

and a finding a True "Self" (with a capital S)

and a connectedness to a

Unity of all things –-

that is the opposite of and even potentially

the antidote to

that meaningless hole inside of

us

Today, I will see that

I'm FALLING TOGETHER

(and falling into place)

(and I'm not Falling Apart…)

———————————

We go through things

sometimes very terrible things

or at least things that are very terrible at the time

that may shift in hindsight

heartaches and disappointments are part of life

but that doesn't make them any less terrible at the
time

when it seems like things are

falling down around us

we have often lived in Aloneness

even when there were people around us

(sometimes we don't see them)

people who have already been before us

and people who will carry us

when we have no choice but to fall

into their arms

and it's ok to fall

they may already be catching us

now

Today

I will TRY TO FIND A BALANCE...

It's easy to see so much of what you don't want and

what you're not getting

what I think you owe me and what I'm not getting from you.

Its hard to understand that my supposed problem

isn't what you're not giving me

but my perspective and "mis-focus" on

what's **not there** instead of what is there.

It was once written that:

"*I am not the victim of the world I see...*"

that the answer isn't "get" or add to me

that the answer is "Transcend..."

Who do you think I am, the Buddha?

How do you really expect me to let go of my desires for

money and success

spotlights and limousines and awards

and sexy times

or even for you to just leave me alone so I can

watch TV and eat a pizza and not have to do

anything or give anything for anybody

do I look like I want to be sitting on the top of a mountain

in the clouds

Chanting "Ohhhmmm...?"

how do you expect me to unlearn everything

when everything we've ever been taught contradicts?

But then again, it was Dr. Phil who said:

"HOW'S THAT WORKIN' FOR YOU?"

"I gave you everything you ever wanted...
It wasn't really what you wanted..."
–U2, "You're So Cruel"

Today,

I will not base my **Happiness** on

TEMPORARY sources

Why aren't you happy already?

Because...

we have become confused

we have forgotten and

lost sight of what is real

My focus is on "(_FILL IN THE BLANK here_)"

stuff

approval

crack

sex

opiates

food

vodka

report cards

nothing that is lasting

but eventually

we'll have to throw out the food in the fridge

that doesn't get eaten

when it rots

and sooner or later

the body will grow old

and the liver will bulge out

because I punished it so hard

and even the report cards

that seemed so important

will get thrown out in a box

with other old papers and photos

and in the end,

when it all fades

what I will be left with

is myself.

Who knew,

that I already had me…

and that that was the best thing

I could ever have

just like Dorothy

with those tacky Red Shoes

the Power was already inside us

all along

(we just forgot or)

we just didn't know it because nobody ever

told us

Today,

I will see outside the

momentary pain I am in

and know that there is another way

of looking at the world that I am not seeing.

sometimes I don't see my life or myself accurately

and sometimes

– not that it's not okay to have feelings

or that it's good to **deny** or disconnect from your
feelings –

I need to stop and **breathe**

or take a timeout

to just put the feelings up **on the shelf** and

reassess with the input of wise people…

to be still.

I can trust that I may see things differently in the light of a

new moment

Today,

I will admit that getting what I want

is more important to me than being

at Peace.

and that on some level,

I don't want Peace

because if I let go and give up

on getting what I think is so crucial

that will bring me value,

I fear I might crumble…

but if I kick and scream

or throw a tantrum

or break and cry and crumple to the floor

a *control* will bring me what I need and then

it will be okay to let go.

That the *"I think I can, I think I can"*

that was supposed to help motivate me

when I was small

and teach me to believe in myself

has become a PacMan inside me

always trying to eat "More and more

and more…"

But I have a decision today:

I could see that I can be okay and Happy

even if I don't get the

"**the** thing"

that I think is most important ---

that "**the** thing" of the moment

(that we are all "*working*")

that I need to make me happy.

But I have a decision today and

I choose:

I will not be the **Little Engine** gone wrong

and instead, I will let go

and just let the tracks

take me.

Tonight...

I will admit to a part of me that says:

I don't want to see Peace instead of this.

I don't want to give to you unconditionally

I want Mine

I want you to give me what I want
and I want to Use whatever I can

the You
the "It"
the whole World

because I am "*Owed*"

and we are the same

whether I pulled you to me
or you came and stayed
here, just to be Free and
to Teach me how
to be not this side of me

to Release
and Let Go.

------

reference Lesson 44
Workbook, <u>A Course in Miracles:</u>

"I could see Peace instead of this."

Today I will be aware that

I am not buying this ring (this car,

this house, this marriage, etc…)

because I love this ring

or I need this ring or

I have to have it

or I will never be able to find one just like it

ever again

I am buying this ring because

– although I may not see it –

I didn't feel good enough about myself

or happy enough

or valuable enough

at my baseline

…before I even walked into the store…

This is not a story about a ring.

*"Debting is not about spending.
Debting is about undervaluing yourself."*

Today, I will realize that

We will reach a point where

Logic can only take us so far

Sometimes my mind and my thinking are not trustworthy…

Broken or self-destructive,

self-sabotaging

even self-injurious.

and often I can see that in the mirror

I am the own worst enemy who lives between my 2 ears

like the answer is sitting in front of your face

and you can know it but you still can't put it into practice

You are no longer my problem

not what you think of me or

my fears of what you think of me

or something that's actually wrong with me

or things I did in the past

I have the information that I am a good loving intelligent person

but I still need help and I will need to reach out

to wise people and

to the energy of the Universe

to contradict and transform my sick thinking

We will all reach a point where

logic can only take us so far.

Today I will

dare to believe that

the world is a better place

for my presence

no matter how things look on the outside or

what kind of troubles I'm going through

that I am just as good as and no less or worse than anyone else

that we are all just equal and that equal is nothing less than beautiful

and that I don't need to DO or EARN anything to deserve to be loved and I will remember when a relationships shifts

when children move away

or a job ends or we separate

for whatever reasons

that whatever the uncomfortable feelings are

it doesn't mean that I did it wrong

I will remember that the wonderful parts that happened

don't go away but remain apart of us and

have gone to make us what we are today.

that at my most essential rawest core

there is nothing inside me but good

even if I have lost touch with this

Permanent and essential Truth

about myself

Today, I will believe this and

mean it.

"I'm thankful for every break in my heart...
some pages turned, some bridges burned
but there were lessons learned...".
---(lyrics from a song by Carrie Underwood)

Today

I will be grateful for my pain because I know

that it will force me to Change

sometimes it is worse to be in less pain

than it is to be in more pain

Years ago, Pink Floyd sang:

"Hanging on in quiet desperation

is the English way…"

And sometimes my pain can be lower grade

and go on and on and last

keeping me stuck because

I am not hurting enough that I'm forced

to do something about it

Today I will learn to be grateful for my pain

and to use it instead of letting it go to waste

and letting my feeling it be

without purpose

The truth is it doesn't matter
what is going on around you

or who is around you
or what they're doing or
not doing

or what they're thinking about you
or not thinking about you

as long as you have you
and you are taking care of business

You will be in the flow
and the rest will take care of itself.

And it will be beautiful in its

unfolding...

"Find yourself elected to a different kind of Free..."
Money Can't Buy It, Annie Lennox

Today I will realize

I do not need completion.

there is nothing I need to:

buy sell own win bank f*#k save

marry own seduce please fool collect

heal impress pay fear hide earn…

There is nothing I need to make up for

and nothing that I need to prove

there is no person who can save or

make me all better

because I am already all better

whether I feel it or it looks like it on the outside or not

I don't need improvement

I don't need saving

There is nothing I need to do

except to remember this

to *really* remember this

(I do not need completion)

Today I will really understand that

before I can Truly SEE

I need to 'UN-SEE'

(what I think I'm seeing that isn't really there)

we tend to fill in the blanks with old Programming that doesn't

apply anymore and though it's easy to say "One Day at a Time"

really putting those words into practice and feeling them in your thinking

is sometimes no easy trick

most of the time when I think I'm "seeing" I'm not seeing

what's really there, but what I assume must be there

or what I need to be there

like when I'm in addiction

that maybe this time it will be different,

or that you hit me again

or that whatever it is that's too much just isn't really happening

or that there are people around us who love us

we need to learn to love even the darkest

parts of ourselves, even the parts we've been

taught to judge, to blame, to revile or even be disgusted with

for until I embrace the parts of me I have rejected

or hated, I cannot move forward or see a

beautiful world

Today I will not control one thing

(or trust…)

I will not be able to do this.

there will be feelings of ugly and
sadness and anger when I see
I can't get my way

that I am a spoiled baby

but I will try to trust that there is a design for my life
that has always already existed within the stone
before even the first cut was made.

And that my only job is to suit up and show up,
take care of business, stay out of the way

and let the great within

be revealed.

Today,

I will let myself see
what I don't want to see

There is beauty in being able to sit still

and allow what's out there in front of me

to be what I don't want it to be and

to admit that it's real.

instead of trying to change you

or getting you to promise to change

or desperately trying to make things be

how I need them to be.

I can get you to promise

but if you don't really want to change

or give me what I want

or something that You don't want to give,

you won't do it

and I can keep keeping myself,

my happiness and my grounding

hanging,

on hold

waiting for you to tell me who I am

and make my life OK.

Or I can see the situation as it actually

is.

Then I don't have to be self-deluded.

I don't have to try to hold off pain

that may or may not be coming later

and I can be free to find out who I am

instead of waiting

for you to tell me.

Today

I will remember that

FORGIVNESS is for Me

(not you)

Forgiveness means release

or to "give (giveness)" it

"over (for)"

so that I can be free

but sometimes I don't know

that that's what I want or

that's what I need

I think that you need to know that you're wrong

I think you need to say that you're sorry

that if the blame can stick

and everyone sees

then I will know I'm right

and that the blame

and being right

and my hurt

can protect me.

On the outsides some of those things can be true

but more important is what goes on

inside of me

Today, I will wish for the

very best in everything for you

(or at least I will try)...

...your Very Best Life

and your Greatest Happiness

(because that is what I want for me)

and if I can't mean it

I will say the words anyway

because I will decide that above all else

I want to be

free

today I will get it...that

FOOD is not Love

(or money sex drugs things fame relationships hurting myself or

a heart in Love or a Heart that's Broken)

and Today,

I will get to the ROOT of all matters

and GET RIGHT WITH MYSELF

I can eat to hurt myself

I can eat to get High

I can eat to push you away

I can eat for shame

but I still have only one problem which is that

somewhere along the way

at some time in the past

(probably when I was small or even very small)

I became convinced that something

was very wrong with me

or that I did something so wrong

(how bad could it really have been?)

that I was unfixable.

And it stayed with me

today, I don't have to prove to you

that I am good

because I am already Good

whether you approve of me or not

and when I can remember the Truth about me

- how monumentally Good - I really am

the Food (or money or sex or drugs or things

or prestige or awards or fame or relationships…)

will drop away or

fall into

right proportion and perspective.

GOD IS MY BOSS, GOD IS MY ACCOUNTANT, GOD IS MY AGENT GOD IS MY LAWYER GOD IS MY MANAGER GOD IS MY BANKER GOD IS MY LOVER GOD IS MY SEX GOD IS MY HUSBAND GOD IS MY WIFE GOD IS MY PARTNER GOD IS MY WRITER GOD IS MY THERAPIST GOD IS MY TEACHER GOD IS MY HUSBAND GOD IS MY GUIDE GOD IS MY COMPASS GOD IS

MY INSPIRATION GOD IS MY INTUITION GOD IS MY WORK GOD IS MY HEALTH GOD IS MY TRAINER GOD IS MY BODY GOD IS MY MUSCLE GOD IS MY HEALER GOD IS MY SUCCESS GOD IS MY HAPPINESS

GOD IS MY STRENGTH
AND

GOD IS MY ONLY SOURCE.

Today I will not assume that other people

are exactly like me...(that you think and process and

feel the same way I do)

even similar people

think

react

process

interpret and

give different meanings

to the same situation

depending on their beliefs, where they come from

and their programming from the past.

We have different values and rules about emotions

and about how we should express them

(if at all)

to know and understand you I need to consider where you come from.

If we assume that everyone is going to be just like us,

then we are going to have big trouble getting along in this world

They say that the people who are meant for us

are the ones most different from "Me"

 - within reasonable limits -

because they are the ones who will cause us most to grow

because they will instinctively know how to push

the buttons that are the rawest and

force me to change.

sometimes things happen that I am powerless to change

I think it will last forever

and that I will take all the strength I have

not to fall apart, trying so hard to mend

the pieces of my broken heart

I may feel sorry for myself and think

that I will always be locked up in these CHAINS

but (today I will remember that…)

I WILL SURVIVE

and the someone loving me

will be ME and I will throw away your key

and I will learn to LOVE myself,

the way I wanted you to…

hey, hey…

Today,

I will not let my MOOD be determined by what's going on around me.

calm and happiness
are not things I need to go 'outside' to get.

They are already within me and available
 to access at anytime.

I need to develop the skill to DECOMPRESS
even when I can't get away to the quiet and remove
myself from all negatives

  (because sometimes that just isn't possible).

Today,

I will stand back and leave you and your Trip over there

I will not step into it

and I will not make it about me

I will just observe

In my mind, I will shuffle through my list of

standard negative projections

and I will check to see if they are already in play here

I will do my best to see what is mine

and what you are actually bringing to the party

and I will realize that I always have decisions about how to

interpret

My experience is the world I see

if I am in attack thoughts
Then that will be my experience

Is that what I want?

either way I will choose
whether I consciously make the choice
or not

Today, when I am confronted with

the acting out
behaviors of a child
(even when they're coming from an adult)

I will remember that the appropriate response
is not to Attack or Punish

but to Love...

whether that means letting them
go to jail or stay in jail
or embracing and holding them
to comfort them.

The people around us are smart.

They know what they're doing and
the effects they're having on us

at least **on some level**
whether they can admit it or not

but aren't we all the same
and who among us has not done the same thing
and maybe "Me" more than most
and how would I want to be treated
in that same moment

of sadness and fear?

Today,

I will realize that I can

BE STILL

and I will accept the circumstances of my life

especially the negative things

as they are

because the more I struggle against what

I don't want and what hurts,

the more upset I will get and worse I will feel.

Instead I will

PAUSE

and open myself to sense the right thought or action.

There will never be a time when everything will line up

and all the elements will fall into place.

I will realize that

this is not an EMERGENCY

The things I don't like right now are not

(most likely) going to last forever

and I can sit still and let go

and make right plans until the time

when it is the time

to make Changes.

today,

I will realize that Change is Inevitable

and I will decide to positively incorporate the change.

We have a life in our head that we believe we have to have

requirements and prescriptions

things I think I couldn't live without…

things without which I couldn't want to live

when I try to hold on and insist
on even childish dreams coming true,

I am setting myself up for pain.

We get confused and think that the things we're going after

or demanding or that we've gotten used to

have become the purpose of our lives

that they have become who I am

but the nature of life is movement.

and when I can get out of my own way

and let go of my preconceived ideas about what I need

for my life to be "Happy,"

I can let Life flow in its own beautiful and wiser shape

around me.

Today,

I will allow for
the tiny possibility that

my present disaster
is what it will take

to get me where I need to go.

I may not be able see it until I get there
and from the other side

and it may be like torture
when I can't

Let go

yet later, looking back
I may see that
even this was

perfect.

Today I will not try to change you(part 2)

I will realize that you are the way you are for a reason

for your protection

or your happiness

by choice or by mistake

or because it's the only way you know how to be

whether you can give me what I want

or you just don't have it to give

whether you can accept the ways I have let you down

or whether or not I can do these things back for you

I will let myself **ask once** because I am not perfect.

then I have choices:

I have the opportunity to adjust myself

to stand by you or at a distance

but in strength, whole and in my perfect Aloneness,

either way - knowing that only then, can I truly

Love you.

Today,

I will give you space.

I will recognize that sometimes the most loving thing I can do

is leave you alone to go through whatever it is you need to through

until you come back around

I can trust and respect you enough to know

that you can take care of yourself

I will let you know that I am here if you need me

and you ask for help

but if not I can let you do it your own way.

I will not make it about me or me not getting enough attention and I will not assume that you are the same as I am,

that you would need what I would need

or that you would process the same way I would process.

I will keep the focus on me and taking care of business

as it shows itself in front of me

which is always the answer to every problem

and I will honor you by giving you

the space

to do that too

Today I will realize,

I am experiencing the
 imprint of the past

you are not the cause of my sadness
  (anxiety, fear, anger, depression…)

and I have become lost in what looks to me

like the present moment

but I am experiencing the imprint of long ago

which isn't really here

and so you are not the cause of it

and you cannot fix it.

I will stop,

pay attention to my breath

and slow it,

listen for the ticking of a clock

or the birds outside

or feel the ground beneath my feet

and let it bring me into

the here and now.

Today I will realize

It's harder for me to see all the many reasons I deserve to be PROUD — but they are there.

There is nothing I need to do to earn "being worthy."

The biggest bump in the way of my life is my struggle

with Forgiving myself.

Forgiveness means letting go.

Letting go of my judgment and rejection of myself,

Letting go of my fears of you

and my beliefs that the world is against me.

When there is pain it doesn't mean that I am doing it wrong

or it's not working.

It's supposed to hurt because that is part of a

healing process.

Today, I will remember that **at any time**

I can UNHOOK FROM MY DEMANDS

to regain my Peace

You and the world may never give me what I want

or you may,

in spite of my fixation or desperation.

what you are not giving me or what I think you owe me,

the idea that you are disrespecting me or taking advantage of me.

I will realize that the only power that these have is the power that I give to them.

There may be some things we may never be able overcome or incorporate.

I need to BE OK no matter what happens.

Even if we part

And when I let go, then a space can open up,

even if its only a tiny crack in the door

that can allow almost anything to happen

(maybe even what I was wishing for)

and I can remember that I have always been

Whole and Free

and you can just live your life however it is you really want to.

Today, I WILL TRUST MYSELF

Someone who doubts themselves

(even when they are OK)

and who can't tell what's real and not real

people who feel guilty

when they've done nothing wrong….

these are usually the traits of people

who have in some way been abused.

The person I think I see in the mirror
is not who I really am….

and

today, I WILL MAKE UP for LOST TIME

Today,

I will remember what is
REALLY IMPORTANT to ME.

It is so easy to get distracted.

Sometimes it seems like we live in a world of

spiritual, financial, emotional and romantic

ADHD.

We lose track of our values and make choices

that betray the person we were raised to be

or should have been raised to be

or wish we could be but may have come to believe

we've lost our chance to become.

How is it that along the road of my life

I forgot about the Cow only to end up with a

handful of

"Magic Beans?" (how stupid could I be?)

but then again, maybe the cow would have turned out to be boring,

and those beans did provide quite an adventure…

the adventure that made us who we are.

When I am clear, I will realize that I'm still getting where I need to go,

even if it's not where I originally set out for

and that the new destination is better

that even if I could, I wouldn't go back

and that backward wishing

is only a waste of time, anyway

and that the wonder of the beans is still revealing itself.

Today, I will realize that right now

is a choice and

I'll take the Magic Beans.

Today,

I will just DROP IT

If I am keeping your love on hold and you

on an emotional trial basis

before I'll put myself 100% all in…

if I am waiting to see if you will make the changes

I think you need to make to demonstrate

whether you really are the one I am looking for or

whether or not you can perform or behave

to **prove…**

then I may miss the beauty and perfection

that you are already radiating and

that you already are.

for you see,

Life is happening right now

and while I am taking notes and comparing,

trying to figure out whether you're GOOD ENOUGH

the moment may pass me by

and

You may pass me by (because you get tired of waiting)

Let me best worry about working on myself,

taking care of business and being the best me I can be,

and just DROP IT

(all of IT),

and let it take care of itself.

Today,

I will not come up with reasons
not to Love you (and I will do my best to drop my exceptions)...

whether you are smelly
or too pretty
or you wear the wrong clothes
or have the wrong politics
or you are too rich or too poor
or too snooty or too religious
whether you're a sinner or
a goodie two-shoes
or you're ugly or too perfect
or you're the wrong race
or too stupid or too fat or too skinny
whether you're a loser or too smart

or too nerdy or a joke
or a drunk or a drug addict

or you left me or you hate me
or you love me too much
or you're too weak or too strong
or too cold or pathetic or needy

or you remind me too much of

me

or I'm jealous because I think you
are the things I'm not
that I think I need to be
  (and then everything would be all right)

Today, I will stop looking for someone to kick
even if it looks like they deserve it and everything
in my external world tells me that it's OK
  (and I will even get a laugh out of it)

and I will release all of these judgments

for you

but even more because they are
oppressing

me.

today I will remember that SOMETIMES EVEN WHEN IT SEEMS LIKE THINGS WILL NEVER CHANGE, THEY DO CHANGE

and today, I will believe it and if it is hard for me to, I will at least believe that there is a POSSIBILITY (even a very tiny one)…

that it is *possible*.

I will remember that impossible situations have changed for other people and I will stop insisting that it can never happen for me even if that makes me vulnerable and I might feel terrified. I will learn the skill to accept there will be pain and I can feel it and when I do, I won't die and I will realize that I can travel the world or try to get famous or try to destroy myself to get you to notice me or to get my revenge on you or to prove you wrong.

but the Truth will always show itself…that no person or outside thing can ever be my solution or save me

My True answer will come from the Good inside me.

Today, I will be willing to try it
SOMEBODY ELSE'S WAY

If my way is working so perfectly

what am I doing here right now?

and maybe I will consider

that this place right now

is the perfect place for me to be

and this is perfect time;

I'm just missing it

I will stop staring in the rearview mirror

and straining to see farther up ahead than

I'll ever be able to see

and for a change, I'll look at the map

and follow the directions

I will sink into the present moment

seeking and opening myself to the beauty

I am missing that is definitely

already here

and I will stop waiting for

a destination I think I need to reach

and I will realize that every moment

and every space along the way

even this one Is

exactly where I am supposed to be

Today,

I will GET OUT OF MY OWN WAY

we can be so creative

and on a daily basis come up with new ways to self-destruct,

to put roadblocks in our own way or at least

pop our own flat tires.

sometimes it's just annoying and sometimes it's more severe.

What if I really wanted to just **get on with my life?** (instead of just saying it?) What if we could really understand
 how wonderful we truly are that I really do deserve good things?

But if I really am willing to take responsibility

and accept that I am the architect of these patterns,

then I can learn to see them and change them

and when I find myself in the middle of one already in progress

I can stop and step out of the situation

and as I get better at it I can even see my patterns

coming down the road up ahead

and when I learn to see them in time

at least some of the time

I can avoid them and I can

choose another road

Today,

I will not WORRY ABOUT TRYING TO FIND THE ANSWER

I will realize that finding it is not my job

that it has already been handled
that it has already taken care of

like the statue already there
inside the granite before it's been cut

and I can KNOW
it has already been done for me
and it's coming...

It's already

ON THE WAY.

Today, I will do what I can

TO MAKE THE WORLD A BETTER PLACE:

(and I will realize that I am already doing it)

(most people are generally doing the best they can

and what they think is right at the moment...just trying to be

happy)

I will do what I can to try not to hurt others.

and I will notice when I am kind and caring and

I will look for opportunities to be more polite,

less sarcastic and less angry.

and I will let what I can do be enough.

and when I do this, I will DEFINITELY see that

the world is a better place than I

always

think it is.

Today,

(for only a 24-hour vacation day)

I will let myself JUST PLAY THE TAPE.

I will not torture myself for hurting or not knowing what to do if I am stuck

and

I will do my best to try to EMBRACE my "stuckness," and know that

- even if I am tired of hearing myself -

I am still a good person and in the middle of it

I will accept,

approve of and even

like myself.

whether the house is upside down

or I lost my job and I can't get a new one

or I can't get out of that same job I hate

or I'm living with someone who's drinking

or I can't stop using

or I've been a bad parent

or I can't take my physical pain anymore

or I'm tired of being so angry

or I can't break away from the family that always lets me down

or even if I can see my patterns clear as day

but I still can't seem to break them

I will recognize that all around me, no one is perfect

and they all have tapes of they're own that they're playing and

We all get stuck in our own loops

(apparently, that's just part of the human experience)

and I will realize, that until I can relax

and let my **insides unlock**

and let myself be who I am

where I am, right now

and that for some reason this is what I'm supposed to be going through

I will stay stuck and nothing is going to change

I can look at it all again tomorrow and I will

but for just one vacation day

I will stop and let myself

exhale

today,

I will remember that
ALL STORMS PASS

I will REALIZE THAT
THE UNIVERSE WANTS ME
TO BE HAPPY

and that

I DON'T KNOW
WHAT THE SHAPE OF
MY GREATEST HAPPINESS
IS SUPPOSED TO BE

what the pieces are that will make it up
what I'm supposed to keep or lose
how I'm supposed to change

or stay the same.

In the times of my greatest pain
it is impossible to believe this
but that doesn't make it untrue.

all storms pass

and happiness will always be a decision
even when I feel like I can't make it.

I can learn to stay out of my own way
no matter what has happened to me
or where I've come from
or what I've done or not done
in the past

and I can let the good inside me
take and carry me

and let that shape be

revealed
to me

Today, I will learn

HOW TO HANDLE CONFLICT

without hysteria

Learning together how to handle conflicts –
in every relationship – by being and staying
PRESENT and AUTHENTIC and not creating
excitement and drama to push us apart is more
important than what happens to "Us" in the
future.

Today, I will make the commitment to stay and
be a SAFE PLACE together as we navigate
through fully.

I will understand that there will be things about
you that I don't like and

I will realize that most of "what you did to me" and "how you hurt me" were already present before you even arrived on the scene.

You have the right to be in this world exactly the way you are whether that meets my needs or not.

And I will know that that's OK because I create ways to take care of my needs myself.

THERE IS NO TRAGEDY here because

THERE IS NOTHING MY SPIRIT CANNOT OVERCOME.

Today I will realize,

There is no TRAGEDY here

because THERE IS NOTHING MY SPIRIT

CANNOT OVERCOME (part 2)

– or -

Today I will not live in the past
or
let my past run my present

sometimes, in the face of loss

the death of a loved one

or the threat that things won't work out

the world tells us that it's supposed to
turn bittersweet

and beautiful with time

and that it will be OK

but it doesn't feel that way in the middle of it

someone once wrote:

> **"and a heart that has been broken**
>
> **will be stronger when it mends..."***(Tom Waits)*

but what if that heart grows stronger

and leathery and closed on the outside

but inside there are still hurting and ghosts

that have never been healed or bled

and that felt so real back then

that it was going to kill you

so often we experience those past ghosts

even though they're not still here

and they distort the looks of things now

and until we can grieve and bleed them out

and allow that **they really were**,

we can't be free to live here and now

and accurately see

a broken heart at 13 or 15 or 23 is not still here 20 years later, and

so right now is no tragedy.

Sometimes things don't work out

Sometimes they do

that's just the way it is.

and even though we KNOW we are supposed to know that

the outcome will be the best one

sometimes **we don't want ACCEPTANCE**

because it means we have to release and concede

to our innermost selves

that it may already be gone when we think we can't take it

but **we can.**

Today, I will **PREVENT THE RELAPSE** and **NOT** go into my **OLD BEHAVIOR**

by doing **WHATEVER IT TAKES**

We have a choice.

And today I will go to any lengths necessary

NO MATTER WHAT

and that means changing my old playmates,

playthings and playgrounds and

If I need to I will get rid of toxic old friends

- even if I love them -

and sometimes even family

and I will be honest with myself

about them taking me down

and if I have to get rid of you

because you're using

or because I can't stay well around you

then I will because blaming you can mean

killing me

and I will sit still and go past and beneath

any cravings that arise and my commitment to

"I can't take it" and into the feelings that I am so afraid to feel -

the sadness, shame, fear and anger

 that are stuck like poisonous barbed

hairballs

and finally,

I will let myself feel and process them and

release.

and I will realize that the problem is within me

and not in the outside world or in anyone else

and I will take responsibility because I am the only

place

where I can make

change.

Today,

I will SIT WITH the UNCOMFORTABLE

FEELINGS (and realize how important this really is)

The ability to sit with, sit through, weather and incorporate

uncomfortable feelings is so much more than we realize.

even when I think "I can't take it"

and it seems too much...

this will literally mean the difference between

success and failure, sickness and health,

recovery and relapse and even

life and death

(no exaggeration)

When I can accept that hurt and

anger posing as hurt

are SUPPOSED TO BE,

and I can't outrun them,
I start to have a chance

that there is no Magic Wand

and this is not an emergency.

I don't need to run or run by attacking.

I am strong. I can take it

and I will be stronger

and when I can say

BRING IT ON,

then I will get better.

I will drop my silly but popular and normal hope

that I can avoid my share of hurt and discomfort

like life is a game of emotional

dodge ball.

Today, I will identify and get rid of my
old ideas about WHAT I DON'T DESERVE (so that I can release them)

My life is controlled and sculpted by my old inner beliefs about what I am worth and what I deserve. But I think it's "You."

We have been trained to be outer focused.

I look at your approval of my performance, my looks, my body, my money, my popularity and I think that you are holding me back or maybe the world is against me…that I just can't win or I was born under an unlucky star.

When I realize and remember how amazing I truly am, then my life will Change.

The world will not fall in love with me until I can fall in love with me
and you cannot desire me or believe in me or forgive me until I get right with me inside first.

And today, I will look to find the **positive**
kickbacks
  (knowing that they are always there)

for this **self-rejection**
  (which I also may not see on the surface)

and which is ultimately **the** defect that I need to be removed.

The Universe is on my side and it likes me. And today, I will realize it's time to catch up

and get with **the program**.

Today,

I will watch the NEWS CLIP only ONCE

whether we are in the middle of a natural disaster

or there is a deadly accident on the other side of the freeway

or a movie star is imploding under the weight of fame and money and privilege and addiction

or a girl named "Snookie" is running around drunk on the Jersey Shore

or someone is being beaten to death in the middle of a race riot

or there might be rain in Southern California...

(some of these things are more important
than others but they are often presented to us as if
they are the same)

I will still be an informed and aware citizen and I will
be responsible

and I will DO MY PART to make the world a better
place.

And then I will stand back and let the madness part
of the

world spin.

Today,

I will release the idea that I can punish you by not loving

you (and I will realize that whenever I withhold love, the one I punish is me)

_____

if the opposite of hate is not love but indifference,
then why do I care so much if you have let me down,
or not fulfilled your promises to me or carried out my agenda?

People have limitations. I'm not very interested in hearing that because

I want what I want. And now, please.

They say that we will achieve happiness when we can release everything and there is nothing that we

need anymore.
That in the quiet simplicity of this, we will experience
bliss and ecstasy...

Why does that sound so false to a Pac Man like
me?

Instinctively, part of us knows this is true yet at the
same time,
there are things I don't want to give up, things that I
know are the
FUNCTION AND PURPOSE OF MY LIFE (that
apparently really aren't)

Today, I will look at the places where I am stuck,
my obsessions and the things that I think I
need so badly
and the rules that I impose on my life and the
people in it
that keep me in my boxes and I will ask
myself whether or not

I really want

Peace?

(if you need to take medication or need to do anything you might not want to to take care of yourself...)

Today, I will take my MEDICATION whether anyone else likes it or not, no matter what they say to me or what judgments they put on me. If someone is ashamed of me, I will let them keep their shame.

If they say "you don't need to take that medication. It's not natural" or they say "WE DON'T HAVE CRAZY PEOPLE IN OUR FAMILY" or "You are a disgrace to this family" or I look in the mirror when I'm doing good and I tell myself "Look how good I'm doing. I DON'T NEED THIS MEDICATION" or if someone clean and sober and well meaning and maybe even wise who I look up to tells me "If you take that medication, you are not really sober."

And if I can't remember whether or not I have taken my medication, I will make a system to keep track to make sure. And if I still have trouble I will ask a friend I can trust to help me with this.

I WILL NEVER TAKE MEDICATION TO GET HIGH OR MISUSE ANY MEDICATION THAT IS PRESCRIBED TO ME. And I will be **RIGOROUSLY HONEST** about this.

I will not be secretive about medication and I will make sure that the SOLID SUPPORT people around me always know and I MUST have those people around me.

And I will realize that pills ALONE cannot be the solve of my problems. If I need to go to therapy then I will go to therapy (whether I am judged for that too or not)

And if I need to go to meetings, I will go to meetings even if someone tells me "What do you have to go to those MEETINGS for?? or "why do you STILL go to those meetings…?" or "those meetings are just for people who are weak."

Today, regardless of what the world says, **I will do WHAT IS NECESSARY to TAKE CARE OF MYSELF** whether anybody else likes it or not or **even if I DON'T LIKE IT** because today I make that decision that I don't want to

END UP DEAD and I do WANT TO LIVE.

today,

I WILL NOT TURN MY DR. INTO "THE CANDYMAN"

and then blame him later if things go horribly wrong.

It is so easy to get a Dr. to give us almost whatever we want

they are caring people and they want to help.

They don't want to see us in any kind of pain.

I have a responsibility for my part in the equation

and I will make sure I get educated and that

I KNOW WHAT I AM GETTING INTO and then

later

not play Blame and

the VICTIM.

Today, I will not let THE QUICKSAND (of my emotions)

TAKE ME DOWN

Some people keep their feet on the ground and
some people live with their heads in the clouds
and for some people normal life can be like

living in QUICKSAND.

Depression, addictions, abuse and failures from the
past
can seem like they're sucking you under and
sometimes trying and harder and harder
only seems to make things worse.
You may just think you're just UNLUCKY –
and that may be true.

But the first thing I need to do it be still and get
calm.

Often, we don't realize that there was a MAP
or that even if there wasn't a map

or no one ever taught us how to read one,
we had a part in at least some of the wrong turns
that took us off the road and that just because

I'm in the Quicksand now doesn't mean
I'll be there forever or that if
I call for help someone can't come along,

throw me a line and help me

pull myself out.

TODAY I WILL LET GO MY EXPECTATIONS ABOUT WHO I NEED YOU TO BE AND HOW I NEED TO BE LOVED

Meatloaf sang: *"..I been looking for a ruby in a mountain of rocks but they're ain't no Coup de Ville hiding at the bottom of a Cracker Jack box..."*

When you don't match up to my picture of you
whether you're my wife or my husband
or my parent or my child…
I can be devastated and I can blame you for it
and I can crumble or rage
even though you showed me who you were
and everything I needed to see when we met

…in the first 5 minutes.

And if you don't love me responsibly
or the way I think I deserve or I "need" you to
it doesn't mean that I did something wrong
or that there's something wrong with me
or that it's my fault.

Unless I am a serial killer
I can know that whatever it is,
it's mostly about you because
everyone has their own trip and
most people are just living their lives
and getting through it the best they can.

No one person can ever give us everything we want
or need and eventually all people will let us down
because they are human.

And that's OK and it's beautiful…

because I have ME and I am strong
and I can rely on me.

And you can't love me if I'm your Vampire.

When I can let go of my picture of you

and RELEASE you to be who you are
and leave you over there, I can SEE

who you really are with all your deficits
and in your fullness and greatness
then I can truly Love you and

RESPECT myself.

Today I will realize

I AM THE MASTERPIECE

and today I will say something so amazingly wonderful about myself that it makes me feel embarrassed to say it…

(even though it is still true)…

and I will FEEL it and admit it's Truth.

What would it take to get me to believe and feel that I really am the BOMB?

And how hard is this for people to do who have heard things like…

"I wish you were never been born…and…I'll give you something to cry about"

or "this is all your fault…" or "why can't you be more like your sister"

or "you are a disgrace to this family…" or

just fill in the **blank**

even if whatever it was was said without words.

When I believe whatever it was and deny how awesome I am,

I am lying about myself and I am robbing the world

and who I am I to hold back the Good I have to give?

but when I put the Truth about me out on the table by saying it –

EVEN WHEN I DON'T KNOW HOW TO BELIEVE IT –

the Universe can work with it and bring me forward into

great things.

But if I just retreat into a corner,

I remove myself from the Flow that makes Life

worth living and good things happen and find me.

Today, I will throw off those old tired disgusting and untrue chains

and I will step into the Light. And I can say:

I am a FRIEND. I am BEAUTIFUL and HANDSOME

and SMART and KIND. I am GOOD at MATH

and I have POTENTIAL. I am a LEADER.

I love ANIMALS. I am the BEST COOK.

I am ROMANTIC and SEXY.

I am the HARDEST WORKER.

I am the STRONGEST and the FASTEST.

I am the FUNNIEST. I can WORK THE RUNWAY.

I am a SURVIVOR and

I am a LOVING PERSON.

In all the world, there is NO ONE LIKE ME.

I am an ARTIST and the

masterpiece is

ME.

(and if they don't like it, they can take it somewhere else...)

Today, I will realize that the Change I need cannot come from the OUTSIDE IN but only from the INSIDE OUT

My mind is made up of goodness but also my fears and the beliefs that I'm not going to be OK, that you are out to get me or hurt me or humiliate me. Or the past will re-happen and I'll relive it again and again.

The solution is that no matter what has happened before, I made it through then and that means that right here, right now and even if I am in PAIN, I have the chance to begin again.

There are PEOPLE WHO LOVE ME. I can ask for HELP, TAKE THE ACTIONS and stop saying that I'm the different case…the exception.

If I try to do it alone and hold onto my old ways, then I will continue to be my own block and my life won't change and it will be no surprise.

If I don't get clean and sober, stop cheating on my wife, stop gambling at the casino or eating or purging or cutting or shopping or acting out sexually or dealing drugs stop working whatever obsession it is I'm working and using to distract me and NOT FEEL or not doing what it takes to treat depression…

I will not find the relationship I'm longing for. I will not have a bank account. I will not have relationships with my family. And I will not have a Self that I can be proud of or a Fullness inside.

So I can blame the World instead about how unfair my Life is – which may very well be 100% True – or I can ask for help and do what it takes for things in my life to Change.

(easier for some than others...)

Today, I will realize that
even if it doesn't come naturally,

I can TEACH MYSELF

to be GRATEFUL
and that IT IS A PRACTICE

---

and although it may slip away -
and come in and out...

even when I think it's not there
or I don't feel it

it is never gone.

When I can open myself
it will return and I will see
that it was only me who

stepped away.

**Today, I will remember that
at any moment,
everything could change**

and

**that whatever happens, I
always have the choice
to see the picture differently.**

I can even see a different picture of it in
my mind
and run it like a movie or
I can put a frame around it or a different
frame
that's a different color...

and I can change the colors of the
picture
or make it bigger or smaller
or put music to it or make it silent or
make the feeling of it louder or less
intense

or see it the picture getting weaker and
weaker
until it's just faded away.

I have tools and I can always learn new
tools
to see my life and situations differently if
I choose to use them

(though sometimes, for a lot of reasons,
I may not want to...)

or I can try to hold on and hope or
control
or to try to make things come out the
way

I want them to because I think
I know better than what will happen if I

LET GO.

Today, I will admit that I enjoy my NEGATIVITY

and whether or not I like the results,
it is serving a purpose for me.

And I will ask where did I learn this?

If I had been born on a desert island and
I had never seen a mirror and there had
never been anyone there to tell me
to BE THIS or not to BE THAT
or what was good or bad about me
or what we should or shouldn't do…
how would my attitudes be different
or my thoughts or feelings about myself?

Sometimes people like to disagree just
to disagree,
to be "CONTRARIANS" maybe because
it's fun or maybe for protection.

There is safety in keeping others off
balance and
being ready to keep new ideas out
especially when experience has taught
me
that life is unsafe and unpredictable.
I learn to live trying to predict and pre-
predict
as much in advance as possible as if I
can avoid
negative outcomes at the pass.

But because of it, I can miss out.
I can withhold my love from you
and I can keep you at a distance.
I can keep myself sealed off from new
ideas
and I can keep myself depressed

or angry
or anxious or panicked while I try

to keep myself **safe**.

We don't realize that turning against you
is turning against me and
turning against the World is also
turning against myself and that
when I've fallen into turning on this axis

 – even though they may be long gone
or even dead -

whoever it was that started this ball

rolling for me **won**

and I may not be seeing that I can decide
to and start to change my orbit and my
path

   at any time.

Today, I will let myself see that

I AM ATTACHED TO MY DEPRESSION
(and my negative emotions) and

I GET SOMETHING OUT OF IT

Sometimes when I get so depressed, I can't fight back. But then when I can't fight back that means

I don't have to fight back.

I don't have to stake my claim and stand up for myself and demand my right to my spot on this planet,

in this family, in this Universe…

and I will ask myself whether I will allow myself
to have and express the anger I've been
squishing down and squishing down
and trying to deny and not feel

or whether I am going to take a stand and
quit taking no for an answer and refuse
to let anyone or anything stand in my way

anymore.

and I will admit that no one else can do it for me
and I will stop WAITING for someone else
to come along to…

and whether I believe it or feel it or not,

I will stop denying that the POWER is
already

Inside me.

WHO WOULD I BE WITHOUT

THE IDENTITY I HAVE CONSTRUCTED

FOR MYSELF...

MY IDEAS ABOUT WHO I AM?

The one who is so angry

The one who has been so hurt

The one who is so crazy

The one that no one understands

The good girl. The Helper.

The bad boy. The Problem.

Who would I be if I didn't have

these ideas (or defenses) to cling to?

Today I will realize
that I WANT YOU TO FIX ME
(even though I know you can't)

_____

sometimes you wake up in the morning
and all you see is what's wrong,
what needs to fixed and what's broken…
like you woke up wearing the

cranky pants.

And you just want someone to be able
to fix it…
the doctor, the mommy or daddy, the
lover
or the dealer…

someone to transplant my brain

and refinance my life because
my heart is upside down and

the terms of this loan are killing me.

And when I'm not getting the illusion
that tells me it's what I need,
I can throw a tantrum

(inside or out)

as if that will make that something
reappear or bring me whatever it is
that I need to add to me.

And you would be lucky not to be the
one
who's close at hand when that happens.
It can be easier to shut down than to risk
putting myself out there and being hurt
again.

It may sound trite, but True happiness
can only come from the INSIDE and

when I am distracted by my thoughts of you
or the outside fix, I'm keeping myself stuck
in a state of

emotional suspended animation.

Today,

I WILL NOT TURN ON MYSELF
(and I WILL NOT SHUT THE WORLD OUT)

_____

Sometimes, we can be tempted
to shut down, shut out, turn inward
and turn away

and often when this comes upon us,
we can be jumbled inside and not know
what's real and not real
and sometimes even what happened
or didn't happen and what was

under rug swept.

Many people who have been abused
don't even know they were abused or
betrayed
especially if there are no bruises or
scars
or worse, if somebody told them it didn't
even happen.

I may not know who to trust and
my alliances can become confused
and blurred and turned upside down.

I may have been trained to focus
on all the ways that people in the world
have left or turned on me and
not see people who have reached out to
me
and who are trying to reach me now.

If this is my story, what I really need
isn't retreat but safe connection and
I don't realize that when I withdraw from
you,

I withdraw from me, even when
you can help me find out who I am.

I can hold onto my grievances about you
– even if they are 100% justified –
and use them to wall me inside my own
fortress
or I can realize and decide that
whatever or whoever happened in the
past,

I will not turn on myself and I will do
whatever it takes and there is

nothing I cannot overcome.

Today, I will use the NEGATIVE and TURN IT AROUND

to grow me UP and into a Higher Version of ME

And if I am met with criticism or Adversity, I will say Thank You and

"BRING IT ON"

because I will happily take it in, turn it around and LEARN and use it become a stronger person

a better brother or sister
a better worker or teacher
a better parent or lover or spouse

a better citizen of the One Race,
the Planet and the Universe,

wiser and more compassionate
one level up higher in the elevator
one floor higher up in the
Skyscraper that is me

letting myself be led forward
into my vibrant

radiant future.

Today, I will realize that when it is time, it's OK to DRAW A LINE IN THE SAND

We reach crossroads.

We write rules about each other that say
who you should be as a wife, a
husband,
a mother, a brother and we don't take
into account
that some things change.

That doesn't mean I should throw
you away

but it doesn't mean I am condemned
to bang my head
against the wall trying to get you to
change to fit me either.

And just because I didn't turn out to be
who I thought I was supposed to be
doesn't mean I should put myself
out with the trash.

Love means it is OK to say 'this is what
I need' and if that doesn't match up,
there is no tragedy. Sometimes, shapes
change or move away or come back
and sometimes they stay away and it
still can be beautiful.

For both our happiness and Peace,
I must release you
whether that means we stay
standing next to each other

or drift.

And sometimes we may change together.

These are the natures of

the waters.

As of today, I will no longer INDULGE in SELF-PITY

How did I end up sitting in this corner
when there's sunshine outside

or even clouds or rain.

Or even lightning to strike me?
 Well, at least I'd know I'm alive

When we've become the shut-in in our
own lives,

it's hard to believe that the Universe wants us to be happy. Where was it along the way that I became convinced

that I did something that was so wrong I'd become **defective**

long past repair and beyond any fixing,

separated from the rest of the pack and

lost from the trail of the breadcrumbs I'd left

so carefully –

convinced that that the world had eaten them to leave me stranded

on purpose

But you can't win if you don't play and

this is your one life.

Maybe if you can't show up and bring you're **A-Game**, you might as well stay home and at least take responsibility and stop blaming that world

and everybody else.

And after a certain point, I need to decide

whether I stay shut up inside my broken heart

with its boarded up windows

or whether I just get on with it and realize

that the world still turns outside and no one gets this

ineffective revenge.

I am the only one who can stake my claim

no matter how many people love me or don't.

I am the only one who can FIGHT FOR ME and I can

make the CHOICE

(– and let there be no confusion that this is a choice –)

to fight

or to give up and SQUAT

in the house that was once my Life

and just STAY HOME

and wait for Them

to FORCLOSE on

my soul.

Today I will remember that

SOONER OR LATER THE TRUTH
WILL ALWAYS COME OUT and

IT ALL COMES OUT IN THE WASH

I can't stop the Earth from turning or
the waves from coming in from the
Ocean.
And I can't think so hard that I can stop
you
from dying

no matter how much I love you.

If a drug addict is trying to cheat the test and win,
he may be able to taint the sample and get that
false positive once, twice…maybe more.
But sooner or later, even if it's not
this week,
the test will come up positive or he'll miss it.
There is no need to worry. It takes no trying.
because

the truth will always come out.

Even when there's been a horrible murder
like the kind we hear about on Dateline
or the tragedy of the Tsunami or even
the mass devastation of 9/11…

beauty and humanity emerge.

Our Spirit can't be killed.
The wonderful memories can't be taken
from us
and nothing can stop the Universal
Process
that's growing heartbeats and lollipops
and roses
and smiles and losses and
beginning agains.

There is a mechanism in place.
And it is Powerful and Creative.
Corrective. Transcendent.
Unstoppable.

So I don't need to

control the world.

Today,

I will make the PAIN MY FRIEND
INSTEAD OF MY ENEMY

My expectation needs to be shifted.
When I have a broken leg or a broken
wrist
or a broken collar bone
I know that it will hurt and that I will be in
pain.
I don't like it but I don't think that it will
just

disappear.

But when the fracture is in my heart
or in my mind and it's not visible,

I think it shouldn't be there and
that I'm doing something wrong.
And that if I knew or could just
Read the right book or
do the right trick,
say the right prayer,
or go to the right teacher…

that the pain would stop
and I would be free

and I wouldn't be punished anymore.

Or if I could wrap my mind around it
or understand it logically
then that would make the difference
and flip the switch. But when it doesn't,
that can make it feel even worse.

Change can be like suspension in the
middle of a storm but we think that we
should only have to scream with the
strike of the lightning
and then it will be all over.

But the trouble is not the pain itself
but my terror of feeling that pain
that goes off like an air raid signal
on my insides when I know the attack is
coming.

But no matter how scary it feels,
this is not real.

That storm has always come to wash
me clean,
the way I've always needed to be clean
and
I am not being punished.

There is nothing I could have done that
was so wrong.

As soon as I can accept this
and learn the skills to sit still,
open myself and listen. instead of
shouting…

"No! No!" or "I can't take it"
and trying to violently will it not to exist,
it will immediately start

to subside.

----

and p.s. - (Vicodin will not cure my
broken heart)

Today, I will realize that sometimes

ALL I NEED TO DO IS NOT DO
THE THINGS I NEED TO NOT DO

And sometimes that can be no easy trick
when it seems like external factors are
to blame
when drama is our food and we don't
see
that we feed on it.

Life brings us second chances.
And third chances and fourth chances
though we miss them like packages
we're not there to sign for.

I forget that the natural flow of Good
is all around me and it's bigger than
all my problems.

Bigger than the money or the job,
the divorce or the romance,
the pain in my back or the disease
of someone I love.

But now is not forever. And the future is
not today.

I forget that sometimes all I need to do is
NOT DO the things I KNOW I NEED TO
NOT DO
to not BLOCK that Knowing Good and
keep my unfitting actions out of the way

so things can work themselves out
as they're supposed to and
let Life take care of itself.

My Miracle is being delivered to me
over and over again in a series
of numbered packages
bringing me what I need,
when I need them.

But I must participate
and when the cosmic UPS man comes
and the bell rings, I need to be home
and ready to

receive them.

Today I will realize that

MY ONLY GOAL IS WHOLENESS

everything else must stem from that

and will fall into place and line up with it

or fall away naturally

when I remember who I Truly AM

even the things I'm so attached to

that I think I want and need so badly

that may be eating me alive

 - though maybe I can't see it.

And the rest will come into focus...

that I am OK whether you come along for the ride

or not and I will again know

the real ME.

Today, I will realize

WHAT I WANT ISN'T REALLY WHAT I WANT

I want things.

A big car.
A big sexy life with a big house
and success and money and a private jet
to jet set me around the world and
into the finest circles.

But I experience Possessions
by spirits that fool and take me over
with poison apple promises
that mislead me to believe these are
really what I want

and I lose track and I forget that these things
are supposed to be means not the ends
and that what I really want is just to be

happy,

to be safe so then I can relax
and just be and sit still
and be unafraid and know that

I matter.

Today, I will accept and really realize that

WHEN I AM USING or acting out,
I AM BEING EXTREMELY DISRESPECTFUL TOWARDS and even DESECRATING MYSELF…

We get so concerned about how other people treat us
or don't treat us, whether or not you are loving me
or giving me what I NEED or what I WANT…

But how can I expect you to respect me,
when I don't respect myself?

Whether it means not buying that something special
I have been eyeing in the window because
I want to buy a car and go back to Spain

-or not hanging out with the friends I know
will be smoking bud,
or cutting myself or calling someone out
when I'm already on probation or
setting myself up to be rejected by one more
someone unavailable...
or isolating myself and not believing

I am worth anything.

And when I do not do,
I will feel so much better than I have
because I am committed to myself
and not acting foolishly
and against my own best interests.

I will let myself have dreams and hopes
for my future and I will stop denying
that when I'm not respecting me,
I am also insulting and even denigrating
you because what we give

always comes back.

Today, I will realize that
SOMETIMES
THINGS REALLY AREN'T AS
BAD
AS THEY SEEM

some days we wake up and life seems
like a Snowball

a snowball that's rolling
that we're caught in the middle of

picking up more problems and issues
and situations
and bills like emotional interest that
sneaks up on you
like a credit card

and it feels like you just can't take one more step
or one more straw on your back just like it really is
"all and all it's just Ay-nother brick in the wall..."

But we are so much stronger than we know
and we have just forgotten...
and if we can get the ball to stop rolling
and start to break down the bricks piece by piece
we can actually deal with most of our individual pieces

-- even the ones that seem most impossible.

Today, I will accept that when I am in crisis
or **think** I am in crisis...

  (*and although these may blur together for me,*

I can learn to tell the difference)

...I will realize that the "Snowball
Effect" will distort
our perspective even though cold hard
history proves
that I can get through anything and
that this is the time
to remember, to reach down deep, to
stand up
and partner with the Universe and say

"BRING IT"

so we can get complete with this
and move forward.

And I can learn that most of the things
I am so afraid of turn out to be
little more than

flakes of my life.

Today, I will admit that it's better
that I DON'T KNOW THE PLAN

I want the directions turn by turn,
the 76 Station on the right and the Dairy Queen
on the way to my future.

But we're afraid of break-downs…
our own or for people around us we may love
who are headed to end up by the side of the road
when they don't have Triple-A.

And when we've been through so many
bumps
and pot-holes and we've burnt out so
many engines
and run out of gas so many times
without seeing it coming

and kicking ourselves after

it only makes it worse when I can't push
my car
out of the intersection by myself
let alone fix the engine when nobody's
ever taught me how and I don't have
any tools.

And sometimes it makes other people
mad
when I'm really just a back seat driver
and
I keep leaning forward yelling and
fussing
and asking over and over

"ARE WE THERE YET?
ARE WE THERE YET?"

wanting to know what we're supposed to
do
and where we're supposed to go and
when
and who…???

and throwing a tantrum when I'm given
the best
(and only possible) answer…

"I'll tell you when we get
there."

I don't have to be put in a corner to take
a time-out

and sometimes, it's OK to just pull over
and rest
and go down for a nap and learn that
this is a skill
and a resource…to take time

(even a short time)
to breathe, go within and listen
or even to just enjoy the ride.

I don't see the Truth:

that I'm really just in the back seat
strapped into my safety seat,
more or less asleep and having a dream
and that

I'm not even driving.

Today I will dare to have a Happy Birthday...

no matter how old I am turning
whether it's 43 or 24 or 83
(or you just fill in the blank _____)

and whether I think or you think that's too old or to young
and or I feel sad or angry or ashamed or afraid or even

Happy (if someone told me I'm not supposed to).

And I will not lie and say I'm 29 again and again and again
or wish to be. And I will have no interest in living in the Past.

And if it feels (and some years it does)
like someone left my cake out in the rain
and everything in my life is melting
and I don't think that I can take it

because I'll never have my chance at that
recipe for happiness again…

I will remember that I have survived everything
and I will remember that I should have been dead
100 times over and I'm still here

and that right here right now
I am the best version of me that I have ever been.
That I know more and I have more experience
and I am wiser and more compassionate and more
feeling

and I know more how to Love…
You and ME.
and I am only getting better.

Growing older does not suck.

I don't want to go back and I wouldn't if I had to.
and I may not know what the right ingredients are
but I can find out and I can let myself be Guided.
And I can bake a

BETTER CAKE if I want to.

Today, I will not ARGUE

with anything
or anyone

and I will not PUSH

I will choose not to let my energy get
away so easily
like drifting out a cracked window
or sucked out the blown out airlock
in an alien movie of a space station
drifting off course because there's
too much NOISE on the radio

   (*there are no breadcrumbs in space...*)

and when I see that smoke starting to
blow

...and it will because there are
   other people in my world...

and I see myself just wanting to scream
or break something or hurt me or
someone else
like there's a little production
of "Virginia Woolf" going on in my chest

I will realize that this is a normal part of it
when I start to try to close my mouth
and the mouth of the negative piece of
my mind

and try to stop living like a frightened
spoiled child.

And I will notice and when I catch
myself and I can get myself to I will do
NOTHING

and I will hold still and be quiet
and circle in thoughts of even just trying

to figure this out until there is a sign or a thought
or a sense of being led or guided...

until I hear the silence and feel myself
drop down into it knowing that in it is always
the Truth I'm seeking.

And I will know that as long as I try
to not force the moments of my life
like moves in a game of "Risk" or "Stratego,"
there is nothing to be afraid of.

my path will always be righted

and I need not live in fear of the words
"*you sank my Battleship*"
as if real explosives
were going to fall from

my sky.

Today I will not give you my Power

I will not wake up in the morning and wait to see…
and decide and base how I feel
on your mood and your level
of acceptance of me

and I will not orbit you like a personal moon
or chase you like a metal rabbit on a dog track.

Today I will not lose sight of my life's purpose
and what is really important to me **for You**.

Whether You are my needle or my herb
or my object or my flesh
or my work or money or my fame
or my lover or my duty
or my position or my role or my family
or even my child.

And I will not choose to live
from disaster to disaster
under constant threats of impending
and looming
and building up "story"
like that old snowball gathering
or grey clouds in the sky
in preparation for the next ear who
comes along.

I will not mistake drama or intensity or
adrenaline for Happiness
even if they sometimes make me feel
like I'm alive.

And I will understand that no matter how
much

I love you or how much any of these
things
may seem to make me Happy,
they can only be secondary,
substitutes at best, even in excellence.

There will come a day
when one of Us will go first.
And then who I will I be left with?

When I remember that
I have forgotten
that who and what I am
transcends all of these things
and that if they should all fall away,
the greatness of the Universe
will still reside in me,
then I will know that I don't
really need any of them,
that at best they have been entrusted to
me

on loan.

And when I remember, then I will be able
to love them all

MORE.

Today I will remember there is ONLY ONE ME

sometimes it seems like we live in
different in worlds
and there are different versions of "Me"
around different people.

That I am like a chameleon.

That there is the me I am with my
friends
and the me I am at home
the me I am at work or school or with my
family
the me in the bedroom or the board
room
or the me in a job interview.

We tailor ourselves to people's needs
for us
and the images they have pre-cut
and the parts they want to see us play.

In the middle of all of this,
it's easy to lose sight of who I am.

Sometimes we go along with it
not because we want to betray
ourselves
but because sometimes it's easier and
even more comfortable to let you tell me
who to be so I can know the parameters
when its harder to have to set them
myself

and then having to risk you not liking
me.

And there are the "Me's" I am with all of
these people

and there is a me watching me with
each of them
And there is the me when I am by
myself

(and I can even be watching myself
then…
never giving myself a break)

Today, I will realize none of these is
the Real Me,
any of these roles I play
(though they may be parts of who I am).

The Real Me is much greater.

Today, I have only One Self and
I will **just BE ME** and

stand

in MY OWN TRUTH.

Today, I will not let my
MOODS CONTROL ME
(or run my life)

Sometimes my emotions can rule me
so I can't tell what's real and not real.
And when they are in full swing,
I can't see outside.

When I'm down I can go very down and
we can go very dark and hopeless and
it can seem like things will never
change.

Or we can get so happy chasing
rainbows

in the other direction and true sexy love
and
crack pipes and slot machines that
I forget about the requirements of my
life.
And then the rent can't get paid
or I lose my job or I end up divorced
or my kids get taken away.

Some other people live totally caught up
in their heads or try to cut off from their
emotions.
But that doesn't work either.

Our feelings came stock factory installed
for a reason. We need them.
They are apart of us and if I don't
learn to come to terms with them,
to use them, to make friends with and
learn to surf them, I will end up

living in pain.

But moods are passing and
I can learn to practice stopping.

I can PAUSE and breathe and
step out of my immediate tornado.
I can get present and mindful
and look at the facts and the details
of the room around me and notice
the thoughts that don't actually exist
here and now that I can't
reach out and touch.

And I can imagine that there is a

possibility that this may be **only** a

time limited disaster.
And with training,

I can learn to see a

BIGGER PICTURE.

Today, I will realize that I HAVE DECIDED TO SEE WHAT I SEE AND HOW I SEE IT before it even gets here

---

When we go to the movies, we look in the newspaper
on the computer to see what's playing and to pick it out.
If I don't like to get scared I don't go to horror films.
Or if I don't like to read subtitles, I don't choose foreign films.
And if we're going together, then we make an agreement.
Maybe I go to a chick flick even if I don't want to because we make a deal.

We don't just suddenly appear in a movie theater
randomly like we were beamed there on Star Trek.

We know what we like and what kind of experience
we're looking for and it's usually something familiar,
that we learned to like in the past...
something we've seen before.

And the rest of our life works the same way.
We're just usually unaware of it.

In relationships, usually, I find you because
maybe you just don't like me that much.
Or maybe you don't even want me at all.

Or I find you because you're too clingy and too
needy
and I feel bad for you and you need taking care of.
But then I feel suffocated and angry because
the burden of you is too much for me to take
and I have to get away.

So I get away.

And we both win although it doesn't feel like it
because we have someone to blame and
we don't have to look at ourselves
which would hurt too much.
And that's what we're running from.

We think the problem is "You're leaving me!" or

"Stop trying to Control me!" or "You're not the Boss of Me!"
but maybe the real problem is that I'm oversensitive to being left and when you leave it "OVERHURTS"

or I'm oversensitive to being used or controlled
so I get "OVERANGRY" or "OVERDEFENSIVE"

and overfeel it all out of proportion.

I *think* that the problem is you but I was already wired
before you ever came on the scene.
I already had the projector installed in my head
and (without knowing it) I was just waiting for you
to show up so I could turn it on.

When I become aware of the movies that are already
pre-set in me to run, stop giving you my Power and realize
that my freedom comes not from getting you to change
but from me seeing that the problem is the
"OVERHURT/OVERANGRY"

in me...

Today I will get it that it's
OK TO BE HAPPY

although we think it's impossible,
like 'Happy" is something outside us
or like an exotic animal from an
endangered species
that we need to hunt
and capture in a net and
put in a cage, and take home

and never let get away.

But happiness is not something we have to
go out and find and kill and conquer.
And sometimes the only thing standing
in the way of letting our happiness out
is sitting still and feeling the feelings
we're afraid to feel and allowing the reality
I think I can't deal with that I believe
will go on forever.

Letting go of fear can be as scary as living
in terror even though the moment of that
letting go itself can be relatively short.

And often, I can even realize
that what I'm afraid of might just be
feeling the feelings
that seem to be taunting me
in a circle around a fire with me tied in the middle
closing in like a game of 'cowboys and indians'
made up of little plastic pieces.

And I can even know logically that this is not real.

But If I can drop the panic and terror of
feeling my scary feelings and sit still
and realize that this moment is

TIME LIMITED, allow them to come,
experience and process...
for a moment it may feel like Siamese Twins
being torn apart inside…

but then it will be over and
have been released
like the quiet of air in a morning clearing.

When I can have the block removed
of the reality I think I cannot survive BEING
or what I think I cannot survive feeling,
I will see that the one who's trapped in the cage

is me, like the happiness I'm hunting
and when I can let go,

it will escape
and that same happiness
will surround and

dance around me.

Today, I will not

KICK YOU WHEN YOU ARE DOWN
(Happy Easter)

We can get down.
Sometimes very low

in gutter downtowns or
on the marble floor of a bathroom in
Beverly Hills

desperate for a way out of Me.

And even if we're not in the gutter,
there are places in all of us
where we feel down or broken.

And when I'm desperate I can need
someone to kick (even if it's me) and
even if I just used to be down

that need can still linger

and maybe without even knowing it
we find someone like us
so we and can kick each other.

The world isn't always full of cheerleading and
support.
We like to humiliate each other and laugh
and call it sarcasm.

And when I rake on you, even though it's false,
I can feel a little better because they're not looking
at me.

But putting you down or laughing at you will not lift
me up.
And no matter how many times you kick me,
you cannot keep me down.

I can decide today that I've had enough
and stop focusing on the suffering and
believe in the Power to overcome
that was installed in me at the factory.

And I can start letting the hard times be over
even if it's just by taking the chance to hope
that I can begin again.

I already have all the resources I need for change
inside me. I just need to clear my junk
out of the way so they can come out.

And if you want to help me, Great.
And if you want to come along for the Ride, Great.
But if you don't, you would be smart not to be in my
way.

And whether you are with me or not,
I will begin the process of my own

RISE AGAIN.

Today, I will be grateful
for WHAT I DON'T HAVE,
everything I have lost,
everything I might be losing
and everything I wanted but I never
got.

It was written that

"but a chair is still a chair...
but a chair is not a house and
a house is not a home..."

and what I need to learn is that

I am not a house or a chair and the
only real home I can ever have
is inside me no matter how much

I love or feel like I need anyone
or anyplace.

And every time something is taken away
even when I think I need it so badly

when I can release it, the **Morning
After**
that they say there's got to be

is

and what I wanted shows itself to be
not so much what I really wanted
and so much much more often than not
what I thought could only turn out to be
my worst most ultimate disaster
turns out to be the 100% very best
possible thing
that could have happened

and though it may be impossible for me
to believe and feel this while its
happening,

I can MAKE A DECISION to know this
logically
and realize that just because I can't feel
it
doesn't mean that it's not true

or that I'm doing something wrong.

the pain is only in the ripping away
which
wouldn't be ripping away if I knew how
to not claw to hold on.

And I think that there are 2 of me:

the one that is fighting to keep the house
and the one that knows it doesn't need
the house
and we just can't seem to get them to
match up

but there is only one me that looks like 2
facing each other in the mirror

and the one I think is me is really just a
backwards reflection that thinks it's real

and the lesson is (one more time)
that I don't need any of these things
and none of them can make me who I
am
and that in time this and my strength
are revealed to me through the

LOSING.

Today, I will DROP THE ROCK
(and keep my hands to myself)

Sometimes we have to give up on
something
or someone and we have to admit
that they're never going to give us
what we want from them or
think we need from them
or what we think they owe us or
what we think we deserve.

And it can be excruciating to let go of an
illusion
especially one we have loved tightly and
the world has taught us we need as a
cornerstone

to prove that we could be good enough
or acceptable
enough to matter and to have a right to

exist.

And sometimes things happen that
really are too much to bear...

maybe the girl we wanted to marry had
other notions
we were presented with sick children
instead of healthy ones
or in business we lost it all
or loved ones were taken from us

Heart Breaks come in many forms.

But if I find myself banging my head
against
a wall or pushing a rock uphill,
I will stop and at least consider that
maybe
it's not moving for a reason

and maybe I'm being told it's not right for
me
at this time and if Life is not flowing
in this particular channel right now
maybe its not where I'm supposed to be.

It's so easy to forget that
nobody owes me anything
and that there is life without "You"
and all of these things
and if my head hurts long enough and
bad enough
(any maybe my body too)
I should always remember that I can
make other plans.

I am still a free agent
no matter what I have
- at the moment - contracted for
and I can never not be.

And I am never a victim
because I always have choices

and I am where I am because I still
want to be

and sometimes it's OK just to give up on
a relationship or even just
an aspect of a relationship
or a goal or a job
or a any piece of my life I think I need so
badly
that's an ongoing struggle

so I can get on with the rest.

And today, I will stay in my own seat.
I will not scheme or "help" things along
or poke you or pass you notes or beg
or impulsively leave or get in the way.

Instead, I will keep my hands to myself
and not meddle in

the Greater Plan.

Today I will go BACK TO BASICS and

look at the effects and CONSEQUENCES OF ADDICTION in my life (still today)

In its most basic form addiction means:
I do it because it feels good
but there are negative consequences.
Yet I keep doing it even though
it gets worse.

And we live in a world of addiction
and TV shows about it
and treatment centers and meetings and books
and interventions.
Sometimes it's a word we throw around
that starts to lose it's meaning.

Today, I will look at what my addictions really are -
whether I want to look at them or not -
what I am willing to give up and what I am not yet,
who I have hurt and who I have pushed away

and how I have harmed myself

and what the likely prices will be for what I'm not yet
willing to stop.

And I will be honest with others about this
and I will not abuse or re-abuse you
by blowing sunshine up your skirt.

And I will look again at the effects that my addictions
have had on those around me. And I will look again
at the effects that the addictions of others have had
on me
in my childhood, throughout my life
and everywhere in between

and how I have been addicted to holding onto
people
who were not or are not there because of their own
using

and how I have been addicted to my focus on
and obsession with others and trying to control their
behavior
so that I can feel safe and not have to look at the
pain of

my inaccurate perception of myself
and the pain I might have to face if I
admitted the possibility that I might be

better off leaving.

Today, just for 24 hours

I WILL MAKE NO CHANGES

that are not already in process **and**

I will "NOT DO WHEN I DON'T KNOW"

Today, just for the next 24 hours,
I will make no changes
about the things that are bothering me most.

I will let go and breathe
and take a mini-vacation.
I will just let go and just do nothing
and I will just take a break
from the situations I have pending
and the problems hanging over my head.
And I will just

put them on the shelf.

They'll be there when I get back.
And I will remember that
'there is no emergency here"
and that it is only when I don't meddle
and don't push or manipulate
that it can become clear
what I'm supposed to do
what is really going on here
and what it means

and what the lesson is
that I'm supposed to learn.

I can screw up the plan
or at least knock it off track
or put it on pause or delay.

I can get in the way of what's supposed to happen.

And I can become possessed with the urgent question
of how do I *LIVE* and enjoy my life now when I cannot
know the outcomes of my problems in the future?
But the worst time for me to act is when
I'm desperate and
scrambling in confusion.

Sometimes I need to learn to sit through the hurting
and
the confused and NOT DO WHEN I DON'T KNOW
to get to the part where I know what to do
and let it reveal itself so it can all start to make
sense.

Today, I will sit still and listen
and remember there really is

a Plan and it

knows better

than me.

Today, I will just
see it for what it is...

see it for what it is
not how I wish it could be
not how I'm afraid it is or will be

let yourself see
just what's actually there
and what isn't

the good and the bad

and the actions that speak louder
and hear what is said and unsaid
both with and without words

do nothing so that

you can stay out of the way
and let the Plan work itself out

even when you're not sure how to do that
or what it means
just do the best you can
and let that be enough

stand still and let it come clear
until **inside** you know

and try to live in

reality.

Life is so strange

when you don't know

something could change

and then you won't know...

"Destination Unknown"
---Missing Persons

Today, I will realize

THE CALLS ARE COMING FROM INSIDE THE HOUSE

and

THERE IS NO EMERGENCY HERE

my worst fear has not yet occurred
and it may not at all
the thing you are afraid of
has not happened yet
this is not an emergency
look around the room

there is no emergency here

and I don't know the future
but no volcano is erupting
the house is not on fire
and history shows that
I can feel like my heart is breaking
even while things can be OK

but I can calm myself down
and then I can see things more rationally

this is a skill and I can remember it…
and not just by taking a pill…
just like those damn red shoes,
I've been wearing this skill all along

Jean Paul Sartre wrote:
"Hell is other people" but maybe
it's more true that hell is the
inside part of me that hates me…

the place in me that hates itself

and what if my worst disasters
were mostly imagined and emanating
from inside me

that the **phone calls were**
coming
from inside the house and to be
free of them I'd have to ask myself

have I been punished enough?
do I really believe I deserve not to be
punished anymore?
And do I deserve to be forgiven?
and if I could, would I forgive myself?
and if I can't, what's

holding me back
from letting go?

Meditation/Thought - Part 1
the ADDICTIVE RELATIONSHIP

Today, I will TAKE MY LIFE OFF HOLD and STOP WAITING FOR YOUR CRUMBS

Donald Trump left his wife Ivana -
a former Olympic athlete, socialite and fashion model
with a Masters Degree – for his mistress
Marla Maples. Later he left he left her too.

But when it happened, Ivana didn't roll over and die.
She became an author and the spokeswoman
for Ultress, Clairol's top of the line hair coloring formula
for fashion conscious women. And she said

"GORGEOUS HAIR IS THE BEST REVENGE"
and *"DON'T GET MAD. GET EVERYTHING!"*

In Al-Anon they say it a little differently:

"GET OFF HIS BACK
GET OUT OF HIS WAY
and GET ON WITH YOUR OWN LIFE."

There are so many ways to leave someone...
whatever your relationship to them.
And we can spend months, years, even lifetimes
hoping that people will come around
who will never come around just waiting
to please and be recognized or even
get revenge and get someone to give
something they just don't have to give.

And sometimes the feelings that were different
in the past change and someone should leave you
when they won't leave you or you should leave
them.

You can't manufacture feelings and sometimes
when they're gone you can't change them back.
But sometimes they can change so it's hard to know
and so it's hard to let go of chances.

But I can stop putting my Life on hold
– my family life, my love life, my sex life...
my hopes we will have a future

For some reason we can forget there's
a great big world out there BEYOND
and I can choose to be a victim or I can start
re-writing my life at anytime even if I don't know
what that should look like. I can make the decision
to take myself off your hook and stop waiting
for anyone to come around and realize that
the "someday my prince or princess" I've been
waiting to come along, IS already here

only it's me
and I am the only person
who can be that someone for me.

And I will get off your back
and I will get out of your way
and I will stop being angry at you.
and I WILL GET A LIFE

And I will no longer settle for your

crumbs.

Meditation/Thought Part 2:
 the **ADDICTED RELATIONSHIP**

today, I will not
LET YOU BE
MY OCTOPUS

I love you but
please get off me
take a step back
your love is like SUFFOCATION

I can't breathe
and I can't get a moment's peace

I have been used my whole life
by people I've had to take care of
who've sucked me dry every time
so no wonder sometimes I turn off

and you're only making it worse
with all that talking talking
like a black hole
like quicksand
like a bottomless pit trying to
suck me in
and control me
til there's no me left

and it makes me so angry

maybe I don't want to talk for a reason.
maybe there are things I've stuffed down
that I want to keep down and your
constantly trying to pry me open
isn't helping

your attempts to invade my privacy
are only hurting your cause
not helping, and they make me want to
shut you out even more

YOU'RE NOT THE BOSS OF ME

and if you can't let me be me
the way I want to be
and do the things I want to do
then you can respect me
and no matter how you feel
that isn't LOVE

and if you keep pushing and nagging
all I'm going to do is retreat into my shell
of anger with everything I need inside
the computer, my iPhone, a blunt
a big job, a pizza, the video games
and a girlie magazine

because you make it so that I don't
want to share myself with you and

I won't be **hurt again**
so I'll leave you

out there
where you belong

(part 3)

Today, I WILL NOT LOVE YOU
TO GET SOMETHING BACK FROM YOU

I'm not loving you to get something back
from you
or to get you to love me

I am loving you for the expansion of
myself
and the expansion of both of us

whether I am the closed or the open

accepting you just as you are
and me just as I am
no easy trick as
I may spend my lifetime trying

today, I WILL HANDLE CONFLICT DIRECTLY and PLEASANTLY

(and I WILL JUST DO THE DISHES)

Most of us don't have great skills for handling conflict.
I think I have to beat you or win or
I'll be less or you can have power over me
or even throw me away.

And the last thing we ever want is
to LOSE.

Why do I want to hold back what I have
to give you and get so focused on what you
and the world are not giving to me?

I don't want my life to be a competition.
My today is not about Wimbledon or NASCAR
or about who should be the one to do the dishes
or take out the garbage.

But we get caught up in it and think its about power
or "I'll wait you out" or "I'll show you."

And if you had cancer and you were throwing up
in the bathroom would I mind so much
about doing the dishes?

And wouldn't those DISHES

STILL BE DISHES?

Today, I will refine my skills and
LISTEN TO MY INTUITION

There is a Voice inside us.
NOT A NEGATIVE VOICE.
Not one out to hurt me or tear me down.
Not one we need to USE to try to shut up
or bury over

but one that is there to guide us.

Sometimes my INTUITION is easy to hear
and access and sometimes it seems like
it's not there at all.

like a radio station signal that's out of range

and sometimes I can think I KNOW IT ALL
anyway so I don't need it and I can

pose

or sometimes I've been blocked so long,
maybe so far back that I can't remember
ever knowing it at all,
so long that I've given up on it,
given up on believing it's real
or come to believe that it's given up on me

but it's still there no matter how I try to slice it
or how many times I have been beaten
how many nights I've spent on the street
or how many Xanax I've taken and taken
or times I've been to the hospital
or loved ones I've betrayed
or layers of ego I've tried to add to myself
to try to convince everyone else that
I am SOMEONE of substance or convince me

or how many times and in how many flavors
I've turned away from myself

  (though I'm not fooling anyone)

But my INTUITION is always there
and even in my most lostness
no matter how far removed I may
seem to have become,
moments of it will still creep in

still appear

and when I can get back to the most basic
tools and use them…

to stop, sit still and GET MY BODY CLEAN
set aside time and LISTEN and

let the blockages clear,
then in the quiet still place inside of me
I can HEAR and I will

KNOW.

Today, I WILL NOT DESTROY MYSELF. Today I WILL HONOR MYSELF: (the story of Chicken Little)

---

even if I want to and even if I'm used to it
today I will commit to not destroy myself
or desecrate myself or even try to continue to

chip away

and I will realize that whatever convinced me I should
did not originate from inside me
but I am now the one responsible for change
and I will get to the roots of my personal baggage
of lies and I will begin the process of
ripping them out.

I will STOP just paying lip service and
wondering out loud
"why do I do the things I do?"
when I won't follow up with ACTION
and I will consider the possibility that
I don't really want to get better and change
because my act is working for me and
people are still buying tickets and

I'm still having fun pushing their buttons

and today I will realize and understand
that before I can give any gift to anyone
I must take this stand for myself
and I will make no excuses and give
no explanations.

The foxes may still be back there and hiding
in the forest of my past but they're not here now
and I will realize that as long as I continue to blame
you…

how can I expect to fly when I'm the one creating

MY OWN FALLING SKY.

today I will **meditate**

med·i·tate [med-i-teyt], verb
to engage in transcendent thought,
contemplation, reflection and/or
spiritual introspection.

today, I will take time for myself alone
 (although I could also with friends)

to go inside and be quiet and to listen

to the sounds in the world around me
large and small, the ones I'm hearing
and the ones I'm not noticing

I may pay attention to my breathing
and my senses – absolutely,
together, or isolating my awareness of them

one at a time, sinking into them as deeply
as I can

and I will feel the presence of
the very life within me
it's frequency, it's vibration
it's circuit

or I will sit and regard a sunset
or drink a cup of coffee
or just be with me, my cat or my dog
or look at the ocean or up at the sky
or up at the infinite spreading of a tree
looking up from underneath

and I will listen for any guidance
or direction that might be there
to tell me where to go
or who to be with
what to say or not say
what to do or not do
when to leave or when to stay

moment by moment
and into the choices and the roads
of my life and which to travel by

and in that quiet
I will touch and know
who and what I really am

and not just because all this would
calm me down...

and if directions were available,
wouldn't you take them? even if you
wanted to take the road

less traveled by

Today, I will thank you for being
my TRAINING GROUND

The Universe sends us the same people in different packages,
different outsides with the same issues and situations and
we know they're not just coincidences.

I knew a woman who had a rotten brother, and then
a series of rotten friends and then a rotten boss
who all bullied her. But she could never stand up
to any of them. Then she ended up with a dog
that bullied everyone but her. With the dog she was safe
and she had the power and she could see.
She figured out what the dog needed and also
that no one could bully her better than she could
bully herself.

When she learned from her dog, the sick people who found
her left her alone.

Or it's the same bad marriage again. The same anger,
abuse, the same troubles with another kid on drugs.
The fear in the wife who's been cheated on and
won't forgive you.
The anger in the husband who can't stop drinking.
What is it in us that requires our being mistrusted or threatened
 or punished?

Suspected or kept guessing, off balance. Begging.

Perhaps She will trust you when you more deeply
trust yourself.
Or when **you** are really ready to trust *her*. Or to risk that
He really could show up and come through for you.
What are YOU withholding?

Perhaps there is more mistrust left in us than we
see.

And what would I lose if I didn't have the problem of you.
What if I couldn't give my power away because of
you anymore?

What if I need to make my satisfaction impossible
because inside
I don't deserve "**it**," so I can't receive it or give it to
myself
so I choose to buy another ticket and ride the same
blame ride
again or I can work it out and graduate to the next
level.

And if Mr. or Mss. Right showed up today, would
you be ready
and would they want you? And frankly,

who cares if you don't like me if

I LIKE ME?

Today, I will identify my
OBSESSION OF THE DAY
and
WHAT IT IS BLOCKING ME
FROM

what am I losing out on
what are the good things in my life that are passing
me by...
that I'm let passing me by
because of the things that the teeth of my brain
were gnashing into before I even got up
or opened my eyes

we all have obsessions and
some are bigger some are smaller
and sometimes they're pervasive.
Sometimes it's the obsession of the day
or the moment or sometimes it's the

big dark cloud that's covered over
my whole life.

but there is another life going on,
my real life, in all its parts and including
the usually many more good things I'm missing
than the bad ones I'm magnifying

did I walk my dog today and if she got hit by a car
how would I feel if I didn't? or my cat or my fish?
Did I call my mom or my dad if I'm lucky enough
to still have them or even just remember them
or anyone (even if there's only one person)
who loves me

did I see the good things about myself
and if I don't have the ability to,
what did I do to learn how?

if I struggled with my job or my mortgage
or my divorce or my kids on drugs or the house
that's upside down, would one of them be worth
the stroke or the cancer or the heart attack

and if I were stricken, would I let my world
stop turning or would I suck ever last bit of life
out of everyday like a vampire
that had been asleep for ten thousand years
finally awake and back in the land of the living

and dying?

today I can look up at the sky and the
clouds all around me

from both sides now and
from up and down
and win and lose and still
somehow I can realize
that I choose what I will recall
and what I think I know

or I can let MY OWN CLOUD

swallow me whole?

I will stop believing in MINDREADING

(that I can read yours or
  that you can read mine)

or that you should be telling me
when maybe I don't know all of the story
or that I can make you explain if you don't want to.

And I will realize that I am not a psychic
or a fortune teller
that I do not have the power to control minds
I am not the reincarnation of Jesus.
I cannot control the weather
or know when it's all going to come crashing down
or even that it ever is
or at least I will realize that these things are
very very unlikely.

I am not a magician and I cannot make you
disappear or reappear with the sweep of a magic
wand.

I can't even pull a rabbit out of a hat

but I can disappear without explanation or
you can disappear from me without any telling me
or you
why
whether we're apart or still in the same room

today, I will realize that I can't control people or
things
with my thinking or wishing or worrying or
concentration
and that I can't know what's going to happen
in the future or
what it should be
no matter how much I care
and no matter how hurt or angry I may be.
My family, my friends, what happens at work.
Our health, the interest rates, my chronic pain
and even sometimes my own denial
(even when I can see it)

someone once said that:

*"serenity is the ability to live with unanswered
questions."*
  (...isn't that special?)

But that doesn't change that I can't make you love
me

if you don't or if the feeling's gone and I just
can't get it back.

But if the Universe wants us together,
it will draw us together and if it want us apart,
there is nothing I can do to force it backwards

but either way, I can stop fighting,
find the BEAUTY and get on its train.
I can change my attitude, my thinking
and even my feelings when I take the actions
and when I make an opening and hold the space
for the Universe to fill…

like a reserved table with a card on it for me
in a restaurant
or a parking space with my cone in it
just waiting for my good to arrive

sometimes even just the crack open of a door to
peer through…

and then the changes will start to happen
maybe not immediately with smoke and mirrors
but I will be different and the changes inside me
will start to ripple out into the world.
And that is when the

miracles will
start to happen.

today, I will be grateful for CLARITY IN MY LIFE

and I realize that if I am asking it of you
I need to be willing to deliver it myself.

sometimes we don't want to know what's really going on
and we're afraid that if we know the truth

we may not able to handle it

yet we always want to know where we stand.
It's our instinct. It's our nature.
Like a little kid who wants that same blue blanket
wherever he goes or does better with the same bed time
everynight. We are creatures of habit and we need
to be able to know what to expect so we can relax
and breathe

but sometimes there are things I don't want to ask you

directly or you don't want to ask me
because maybe I'm afraid that if I just come out
and say it I'll find out that you don't really like me
or I'm not who you want me to be or I'll have to leave
you
or vice versa

whether you're my family or my boss or the cashier
at the hardware store, I just don't want to have to
address it.
It's just easier to turn the other way.
But then I pay a price. Living in ambiguity just
because
it's easier leaves me with consequences.

When I turn off my voice, I keep it in and I go into
hiding
and living in hiding is a difficult place to be.
I can forget how to really talk…
to talk about what's really going on inside me.
And then I can disconnect from me
and then my habit becomes I disconnect from you
because it's just safer and I don't have to risk.

Today, I will commit to remembering, investigating
and saying out loud and clear where I stand
and I will have the courage to require the same
from you

instead of watching my center
fade more away

like a chalk mark in a

rainstorm.

Today, I will remember again
that I AM still an ADDICT

———

and what that really means.

it is so easy to forget or tell myself
I am just someone who likes to have
too much of a good time too often.
something to dismiss or laugh about.
but today, I will realize the truth

that I am a child that never grew up
or a child who is now preventing himself
from growing - creating wasted future time.
that I can live at the mercy of my moods
the case of "developmental immaturity" with
skewed senses of self-esteem, boundaries,
what's real and not real, moderation and sometimes
what's right and wrong.

And I won't know most of this until my eyes
have been opened usually for a long time.

I will believe or try to believe that I am different
and that because I have stopped for a short time
or even for a longer time that that's all I need to do
and that "I've dealt with my Problem. Why can't
you?"

that I don't need to look at myself or work on myself
because there's nothing wrong with me.

And now that my medicine is gone,
when I am uncomfortable, I will start to look
for more exits for my blob to ooze into
to give me a little numb to take the edge off
and I will control and immerse and avoid
and I will go away and I won't see it as a problem
because maybe it's not the same drink or a needle
or a pill

and I will make promises and I will forget
the jams I've gotten myself into in the past
and in the in-between times
I will let fade the hurts I've brought to others
and to myself and start to believe hopefully
that maybe this time it will be the time.
And when it turns back upside down,
I will feel like I am the one being victimized
when I didn't do the work that was laid out for me
because "IT" wouldn't work for ME and
I am not like *"THOSE PEOPLE"* when I am

THOSE PEOPLE.

Today, I WILL HAVE A PROGRAM and
I will follow it to the best of my ability

They say that sharks never sleep but really they just never stop moving. And even when they do sleep they need to keep moving in order to breathe because if they stop moving they stop breathing. And people are the same way, although we may find that idea offensive, all only doing the best we can to try to SURVIVE

that is why we need to have a Program in place when hard times hit - a plan of action that's already up and running and pre-kicked in that I don't having to think about including people around me I can have faith in who want to help me recover and who will help carry me when I think I can't move and I think I can't go on.

But just for today, I WILL NOT LAY DOWN AND DIE. And just for today, I will have that Program and I will follow it to the best of my ability even if I do not do it perfectly. I will keep my thoughts on my recovery, in the present moment and on enjoying my life WITHOUT USING – no matter what my drugs of choice may be. And just for today, I will learn to accept and love myself as I am and know that no matter what I have or have not done I am a GOOD person. I will ACCEPT this COMPLETELY -- that I have always had ONLY GOOD INTENTIONS no matter what anyone else thinks or how things may appear to them. I will let myself KNOW that it is True: I have done the best I can and there is no more I can do than that and I will forgive myself because everyone deserves a second chance and I'm no special exception.

Maybe sharks are misunderstood and they're no different from bunnies or doves or puppies and we all need to keep moving so we don't get eaten alive and maybe we will all always have someone or something chasing us whether it's a shark or the past or the brainwash of a family or our fear of the future. But today I will choose to keep moving including the moving that means sitting still and asking for help and listening

in the quiet **for the answers.**

Today, I will just STAY IN TODAY

JUST STAY IN THIS ONE DAY
and if I am tempted to go away from it,
I will pull myself back and I will not go…

"Just for today I will try to live through this day only,
not tackling all of my problems at once.
I can do something at this moment that would
discourage me if I had to continue it for a lifetime…"
  (Just for Today - #10)

and today, I will not try to tell the future. And I will realize
that no matter how hopeless things may seem,
everything can turn on a dime as it has for most of
us many times.

We can never know what's going to happen
even when it seems like we could be about to lose
everything
that I'd never see my grandchildren again,
that we could fall to ruin
that you would have to pack up your house
and load up your car and drive off into the desert
to start over maybe stopping to get a job at dusty
diner
with a loud mouthed fry cook and a sassy waitress
with big hair

your life fluttering up like torn off pages of a daily
'Far Side' calendar flying up into a tornado of
laughter
mocking the sum of your life. And then add to all
that

the word 'forever.'

Or I could realize that none of that is happening
right now
or at least it hasn't happened yet. Not just for today.
And that there are **always** chances that unseen
solutions
may come

and if you knew that the executioner was coming
tomorrow
or that you were scheduled somehow otherwise to
ascend,

would you spend the day falling into the love of the ones
you've been gifted with about you
or would you spend the day picking out your clothes?

And what if maybe…just maybe death got a flat tire crossing the desert

on the way?

Today, I will realize that there is

MORE TO ME THAN MY PROBLEMS

———

(though sometimes I think that I am made up of them)

A very wise and beautiful young girl who
like most of the people I encounter
didn't know how beautiful and wonderful she was
said to me something like:

"I know that we think we are our past
and we are not our past but sometimes it seems like
we are nothing but our checklists of wounds.

And I know that all those events in my past are just
events

and I'm still **Me** but I haven't accepted this into me
logically. But I'm still glad because even just having
that knowledge in my mind is good because
I didn't have it before…"

And then we talked about these ideas:

Just for today I will try to be happy,
realizing my happiness does not depend on
what others do or say or what happens around me.
Happiness is a result of being at peace with myself.

and Just for today I will try to adjust myself
to what is and not force everything to adjust
to my own desires. I will accept my family, my
friends,
my business, my circumstances as they are.

And then I thought, *what is the #1 problem that is
hypnotizing me today* **that I cannot see my way
through**
that for this 24 hours I am letting define me?
And was it the same problem yesterday, the same one
on the same date last year?

We base our happiness on the approval and
acceptance
of other people, on our achievements in the world,
and the attention we get because we don't know
that

without it I'm still great and I'm still **Me.**
So we become desperate and we try to scramble
like dogs on the ice listing and listing and trying
to change it all to fit me for my safety and to change
the forces of gravity and the laws of time and space.

It is so hard for us to believe that the railroad tracks we need
will appear in time and that I will get through
just like I have so many times in the past
and we'll see it when we see it when we're already
on the other side and into the new groove
and rolling and the tracks really did arrive.

And then I told her that she was right.
We are not our past and we are not our checklists
of wounds although it is so easy to get this confused.
And that often I don't feel it and I still haven't completely
accepted this into me *logically* but even having
that knowledge in my mind is good because
I didn't have it before.

And that— beyond all the wounds and lists,
our only Center and REAL CONFIDENCE
is knowing **My** True Identity and the real laws of

gravity and space-time.

today I will carry my

directions for a
panic attack <small>with me in my pocket</small>

---

this feeling is temporary

it came yesterday and I thought it was important,
that it was an emergency
and I felt like I was going to die.

But it didn't really last that long
and I was OK
and then it was over

but I couldn't see til I was outside.

Next time, if it comes again

(1) I will stop and remember that
it didn't last forever and I made it through
and I will make it through this time

and (2) I will stop and see and observe myself
and my fear of feeling the real pain underneath

and (3) let that drop

and (4) feel the real feeling fully
so it can move through me
and dissipate and pass.

And maybe I will even carry this stupid poem
with me so I will be

ready.

today I will commit to
SURVIVING THE HALL

———

There are times when
Life gets put on hold

like during final exams
or when someone you love is in surgery
when your life temporarily stops
or you have to set everything else aside
until it's over

or you're in jail for a DUI
or you're looking for a job
and looking and looking
and you can't find one
or the last minutes before the epidural
when you're having the baby
if you're unnatural

or in the last days when you know its
time to go

everyone always says,
in these times of suspension, that
"you're gonna be OK"
which in those times doesn't always feel
very comforting, and
that's when I want to pick something up
and hit them in the head with it
or throw it across the room

and they say that
"when one door closes
another door opens…"

but it's that time in between…
between the one door and the next
when you can't see the new one
when you're just stuck in the hall
and the hall feels like a terrible terrible
place to be

I can intellectually know that on the
other side of the door, all will pretty much be well
but we can't usually know it deep until we get there

and sometimes in the hall is the time
where we feel like we could just give up
like we can't take one more step
like we could just lay down and die

and it's there in the hall where we must make the
choice

and if we just keep putting
one foot in front of the other
and keep moving and hang on
– even when it feels like we can't –

even if it's just to find out what I chose
behind door #1...

just one foot in front of the other
and soon you'll be walking out the

DOOR.

Today, I will not be a case of my own

MISTAKEN IDENTITY
(underneath the bandages)

There are old movies with actors like
Humphrey Bogart and Joan Crawford in which
the main character has been in a terrible accident
and has to go through an operation.

And when the bandages are taken off
they look like a whole different person on the
outside
even though they are the same person on the
inside.

And sometimes in real life, it happens the opposite
way too.
People change on the inside but still look the same
to the rest of the world and everyone around them

so no one knows.

And Life can be like that sometimes
and it can be easy to lose track of what's important
and lose track of who I am
and that the most important thing to know
is who I am underneath the bandages
and before and after
no matter what anyone else thinks or says
or whispers

so that I don't become a
case of my own

MISTAKEN IDENTITY.

Today, I will be GRATEFUL FOR MY MONSTERS

(the one I AM and the ONE THAT'S
CHASING ME)…

Maybe there is a reason that Dorothy didn't know
to click her heels together 3 times until the end
of the story.

Maybe it wasn't her time to go home yet.
Maybe she had more to do.

And maybe if she had known she would have fallen
in the poppy field while she was running and
accidentally overdosed and never made it up again,
or made it to the Emerald City

or found herself after all.

Scarlet O'Hara didn't rip down the drapes
and make a dress out of them because
things were good. And without Darth Vader,
there is no story.

We need Michael Myers banging
on the other side of the door
or too many children too feed and a crop
that won't make it in on time and a farm
that will surely be lost

and today, I will love my story…

even the ugliest cheapest parts of it because

it is making me who I am and that 'who I am'

is SOMEONE WORTH BEING and
whether for the moment it's

up or it's

down…at least I'M

MOVING.

Today, I will not **SEEK**

NEGATIVE ATTENTION

and I will be aware and catch myself when I am
doing it
and I will stop it in its tracks

and I will not say back to you like Pee Wee Herman,
"I know you are but what am I?" or
"I'm outta control and I do what I want.
Screw you guys. I'm going home!" like Eric
Cartman.

And I will not sit in the window of an old mansion
in the same yellowing wedding dress I had on
when you left me at the altar as a girl
and I made the decision that my life was over
and that happiness could never come for me again.

And I will not sit in a crack house sucking on a pipe
selling my life down the river not even knowing
I'm trying to get revenge or show YOU
or kick it with my homies smoking bud and
thinking I'm funny and thinking I'm not doing
the exact same thing, missing the point
that I deserve better for myself
(even if I need the anesthesia).
And I will not sit in the hall or break chairs or scream
or blow spit balls during class or poke at you
or humiliate someone else or hurt myself
or get myself arrested again because I will realize

that **I DESERVE BETTER.**

Maybe I didn't get what I wanted or what
you should've given me but I will not blame my
problems
on the rest of the world even in the times
when I feel like the pain is so bad I can't move.

The pain is real and no one can take it away from
me.

But I will realize that acting out will not get you to
love me
but will probably push you away. And if you do still
love me
it will be in spite of my behavior not because of it
and I will be lucky that you have seen through my
unconscious

"act" instead of missing my request to be loved
and I will realize that that's all any of us ever really

wants anyway.

today, I will pay attention to whether

I am KIND or UNKIND

and for 24 hours, I could make a list of 2 columns
to notice myself throughout the day
to make a check mark in either one to see
whether I am being kind or unkind…

kind	or	unkind
nice	or	mean
supportive	or	unbalancing
on the same side	or	against
trusting	or	defensive

or you get the idea…

And I could set a timer to go off
every hour at the same time and
freeze and notice myself and my actions
and my thinking and even the postures
of my body.

We are making these choices every moment
in our words towards YOU and towards MYSELF.
And even if I notice later that every mark
has fallen into the negative column
(though I could be surprised either way)
I will understand that it doesn't mean
that I am a bad person, but that it's just a reflection
of my **STRATEGY**, one that I learned
somewhere along the line and not alone,
and I will ask myself whether that's working
or not working and I will look around
at where I am and at the results I am getting.

100% of the time, if I'm unkind,
it's because I'm afraid --
afraid that you'll hurt me or embarrass
or damage me
and I don't realize

you can't take anything Real away from me
 because **nothing Real detaches.**

And in the end, isn't it the people
who are the kindest to me
that I gravitate towards most,
that I am drawn to and make me feel safe
and warm and whom I want to be around?
and even make me radiate from the inside
and believe that I am good and acceptable
just the way I am and bring out
the best in me.

And maybe I will realize that for me too
this is my only purpose in

this world.

today, I will LOOK FOR WHAT I AM MISSING

It's so easy to see what's not there
and not to see the Truth that is there.

I need to be my Earth and not your moon.
I was not born to orbit. But it's so easy to forget,
even though in the extreme this can kill me

 (whether you're a bottle or a pill or a lover or my self-pity).

and there is nothing more appealing than playing
with fire,
compelling like a snake charmer blowing simple
music
and making you dance. Maybe you're all I've ever
wanted
or all I've ever known or all I think I've ever owned.

But what do you do when you put it down?
What are you left with?

But I'm seeing what's not there,
what you're not giving me or doing for me
or what I'm not getting or even how
you're out to get me when you're not at all.

my eyes distort what's in front of me
but when I live and take the
actions knowing logically

then it will start to transform.

Sometimes I need to give up and accept
that I can't see in order to start to see.
And my losses become part of me
and make me stronger and what was so painful
and frightening and what happened
become just what happened,

just the facts,

right before my very eyes.

Today, I will believe that
before me

this is not a person

who **wants to hurt
me.**

This is a person

who **wants me to be
happy.**

(no matter what I see and even if I feel like I have to
pretend)

Today I will let the time come
TO JUST BE DONE WITH IT

―――――

When we think about dragons we think how they
can breathe fire.
That they are impossible to defeat yet we are
charged with
defeating them.

And of course, we all have our own personal
dragons.
Some legends say that from the air,
dragons can see the future.
But some of us are already too good at seeing
dangerous futures that don't exist.
But wouldn't it be wonderful to have those kinds of

powers?

But in all of our lives, eventually the day comes
that we've been so afraid of when it all comes
down to this.

When you have to stand up and face it,
and stand your ground and stand in the truth.
And when it's over, you may be a little charred
or rough around the edges but usually you find
yourself
surprised that you never knew how much you could
do
or survive or that you would feel so much better
after
and so free.

But you couldn't have known til it was over.

That you actually **needed** it and that it had called
you.
That maybe there was a personal dragon waiting,
sleeping within you and that we never knew
we had those same magics inside us and that
I was the one already

breathing fire.

Today, I will use
POSITIVE AFFIRMATIONS

because they work

  and because negative affirmations work,
too…

even if I feel stupid about it sometimes and I think
they aren't working (because I don't see the results
immediately - NOW!)

and I will learn methods to change the ways
I think and talk about myself inside and out

like hypnosis or self-hypnosis or sticking up
post-it notes or signs taped up all over the house
or making collages or drawing pictures of my goals
or going for EMDR or using meditation or prayer
or working the Steps or going to meetings
or saying the right things out loud in the mirror
a million times if that's what it takes
or screaming them loud in the car or in

the middle of a field or copying them over and over
with pen and paper or just saying them out into the
air

over and over and over again

and I won't expect them to work like an instant
Magic Wand
because it just doesn't happen that way and this
process
usually takes time and I will realize that I am
supposed to feel frustrated and maybe sad and
angry
and discouraged along the way and that is part of it
and that doesn't mean it's not working.

I will take responsibility and get it that
I can let my life and who I am tumble like
a random roll of the dice or I can choose
and select and think about what I want
and what I don't want to have

and be

and I will realize that with work,
I can change my mind,
my brain, my thinking and my

OLD PROGRAMMING.

Today, I will recognize that **LIFE IS NOT ABOUT WHAT HAPPENS TO YOU. LIFE IS ABOUT WHAT YOU DO WITH WHAT HAPPENS TO YOU.**

During the Olympics,
in the winter,
on the ice when you are
skating and you

fall…

and you have prepared your whole life,
for this moment
and all the CAMERAS are on you
it would be like time stops

and then it seems like what's happening
starts to happen outside you
and nothing else exists and then you're

falling into the future

and which way it will go

to keep falling again and then maybe even
again in a chain reaction because you are so
shaken
and your confidence is broken
or whether you can pull back into your center
and upright yourself and
drop back into the flow and
continue seamlessly like you'd never
missed a beat

and leave it behind

or you just end up just sitting there
on the ice and you can hardly breathe
and you can't even wrap your mind around it…

there for the whole world to see.

But every fall is meant to happen and
I ALWAYS have a decision to make about
what to do with it.

And what if you had fallen so hard
and you were injured so badly that
you could never compete again?
And what if you became the greatest teacher
there had ever been and it brought you
more happiness than you knew
you could contain and you realized you
never really knew
what you wanted (in the first place)?

or what it really meant

to be happy?

Today, I will not be a
STRANGER TO MYSELF

The truth can be a dangerous thing,
like those old words "watch out what you wish for.

You may surely get it."

And sometimes I don't even tell you or me
because I want the "truth" to be 'better' than it is
and to come wrapped in a bow like

a box of chocolates

where you always know what you're gonna get
and there are no disappointing centers.
But it doesn't work that way.

Reality is more like 'it is what it is' and sometimes
the pieces of the puzzle don't fit in the same shape

that they used to and we may have to pull them
apart
to see how they fit together now after time
and change and heartache.

Sometimes they can make a new picture that's
better
and sometimes we can be ready to be done with the
puzzle

because we've just had enough.

And sometimes we want to try to
put it back together
but we're afraid because we don't want to live
through
one more disappointment, one more hurt
when we promised ourselves we'd never let it
happen again.

And sometimes we don't know.

But if we don't look at the pieces together and try to
see
how they might fit or don't and say it out loud,
it will all surely just fall to pieces.
And that will be a choice.
And I can fall to pieces along with it
or not if that's how it goes. And that would be a
choice too.

And a long time ago, a piano man sang:

"Well we all fall in love but we disregard the danger.
Though we share so many secrets. There are some
we never tell....
Why were you so surprised that you never saw the
stranger?
Did you ever let your lover see the stranger in
yourself?"

and we wonder, *should we be afraid to try again*
when it can seem like you're become strangers?
And it's so easy to say I don't need you and I'm fine
without you yet the feelings just don't match up.
And I can even know all of this intellectually
but inside all I want to do is

ask the Stranger to

Come in from the Rain.

Today, I will not let my

OLD PROGRAMMING GET IN THE WAY of my LETTING GO

———

How do I surrender and Let Go and accept
whatever the results are when I don't meddle
or manipulate and get in the way
of the Plan – no matter what the feelings are?

And if the feelings turn out painful
and I have the urge to act or try and push
and change it then, can I still put my hands down
and let it happen?

It's harder to 'surrender' when parts
of that old programming are still there at times,
when I think you're out to get me
and you can't trust anyone

and I don't believe it when you're nice to me
(for because I am broken, I don't have room
for you to be imperfect or let me down and
I take everything personally)

or I think you will leave me, even when you're here
if you just look at me the wrong way
on the wrong day because I think

I don't matter.

And sometimes it seems like
no matter how hard we work
pieces of that Programming are still there.

But I have a choice.

I can wait forever, for all of that programming
to be gone and for those tapes to wear out
or break or I can learn to live with
what's left of them while they're being more erased
and learn to compensate and do the best I can
and just live my life

and know the lies I'm carrying and see it
catch myself when they're tricking me and
in play and not let them run my life by

remote control.

Today, I will **NOT**
TRY TO MAKE SOMEONE DO
WHAT THEY DON'T WANT TO DO

even if it hurts now,
when you don't push…

because if they do
and go along with you
you will pay a price later

maybe small
maybe high

and it can hurt much much more.

You can only be who you can be
and I can only do what I can do
and if that's not good enough for someone else

you're better off to just let them

be.

Today,

I will **count** the number of people

I can catch LYING TO ME

and when I do, I will count

the number of **lies** and

I will write them down
and number them

and I will keep the list

close to my heart.

Today,

I will **count** the number of people I meet
who **TELL ME THE TRUTH**

or say something good to me

or try to support me or be on

or stand by

my side

and I will write these down and list

and number them too

and I will think about whether I am missing

any of these

or letting them pass me by and I will

ask myself why?

Today, I will LET IT BE OK FOR
YOU
NOT TO LIKE ME

and If you don't like me, that's fine…
Don't like me.

But don't try to like me or want to like me
because you think you should.

Let's just save us both the scene and the drama and
the time
and realize that everybody has the right to be who
they really are
the way they really want to be

this time around on the planet

without critique or alterations or revision.
And if it happens to match up in a way that fits,
that's great. And if not, that's OK too.

Because I don't need you to like me.
You are not my oxygen although
sometimes I get confused
and if people want to change each other
then **maybe that's a bad sign.**

But I'll be free either way
—and you won't need a GPS—

out in the world or still home with you,
together
because I'm **not hiding** and
you'll know where to

find me.

Today, I will Enjoy because
IT IS GOOD TO BE ABLE

TO SIT BACK and see that YOU HAVE ACCOMPLISHED SOMETHING

---

whether it is making it through the
6th grade
when you had a mean homeroom
teacher
you used to be afraid of

or graduating from Law School

or walking with your Mother through the
experience of her death

or building the Taj Mahal (because sometimes
even our small piece of a much bigger whole
can be a completion)

to be able to say that I showed up to do something
and I kept showing up to do my part
whether or not I have something in my hand to show for it

or whether it's just what I have inside. And I can let it

radiate.

Today, I will let myself believe THAT
MY FUTURE HOLDS GREAT THINGS

and today, I will let myself believe that

TOMORROW,
I COULD BE STEPPING INTO
SOMETHING BETTER,
MAYBE MUCH
BETTER, BIGGER

AND MAYBE EVEN HUGE.

And I will say it out loud
even if the fear starts to come up

at just the thinking it could BE,
of the pre-feeling the loss and even
despair
of just hoping or thinking of taking
a risk because I've been disappointed
so many times,

fueled from my past
but not by my present moment.

but: *"there is a possibility..."*

Today, I will consider that

MAYBE YOU WERE NEVER REALLY GONE

I spoke to an old friend of mine yesterday.
We hadn't seen each other in over 20 years and our friendship
had ended badly even though she was that kind of friend
you could instantly feel like you've known forever or
like "in a previous lifetime."

And I'd forgotten after all this time
not only her wickedness but
what good friends we had been
and how hard she could make me laugh.
And I thought I would never see her again.
And as we were talking and laughing again
so hard that I almost fell on the floor
she reminded me of the tired old story about:

"Happiness is like a Butterfly and

if you are always chasing it, it is always

just beyond your reach. But if you can be still

and sit quietly and let it go, it may alight upon
you...."

And we laughed at the other joke version of that
story that goes

"If you love something, set it free.

If it comes back to you, it was meant to be.

and if it doesn't, hunt it down and kill it..."

Sometimes people come into our lives
and sometimes they leave.
And sometimes that butterfly will find you again
and sometimes it won't. But there are some people
you can never be separate from
no matter how physically far apart you go
like the lyrics of a good theme song from a
bad movie that go:

"I'll keep apart of you with me
and everywhere you are,
that's where I'll be..."

And there is always truth in this for all of us.
Some people will be a part of us forever
even if we never see them again.

But the truth still remains, I can't really love you
until I don't need you and I **can** make it on my own
and when I do,

then I'll really have something to give.

It would be nice if life were only like the insides
of a Hallmark card but it's more complex
and shaded
and uneven. And although this can bring you pain,
in the end that's also what makes it more
beautiful....

and maybe sometimes you can pick up
where you left off just like you'd

never been gone.

today, I will let myself SLEEP,

leave the PAST IN THE PAST
and I WON'T BELIEVE MY OWN LIES

I woke up this morning but my head
had already gotten up before me.
And it was hard at work, sitting
at the work table thinking and planning
and scheming and typing and adding
and preventing disaster and missing out
on the good things and the good people
around us…

but not sleeping.

Because I am seeing out of the past
where I learned to believe lies
about the nature of life and people and
who and what I am.

And the lies to you weren't as important
as my lies to me because usually I don't know
I am a liar.

But we ALWAYS do what our system
thinks

we need to do to survive and
all even before I'd even
made the

COFFEE.

Today, I will believe that the Universe will

come through with the PAYCHECK
AS LONG AS I SHOW
UP AND
DO MY PART

We try to keep parts of our lives in compartments.
We try to separate and contain them trying to control them,
trying to maintain them and trying to keep ourselves safe.
Like glass shelves in a china cabinet with crystal statues
or like a doll's house with little drawers I've padlocked
and locked down and stuffed full of fears and the ones

hardest for me to believe the Universe can
or would help with.

Like with money, or the paycheck or with the bills
or the romance I'm longing for, or trying to hold onto
or the ugly divorce that feels like it's tearing me
apart
or the chronic pain in my body or not the un-lifting of
the anxiety and depression of my mind or losing
or keeping that house that's upside down
or moving forward beyond the places where I've
been
most stuck before that I think make me ME but
do not have any such power to make anyone a Me at
all.

But I can let myself be guided.
And I may know when it's happening and I may not
but likely both will be part of the process.
And if it doesn't happen the way I think it needs to,
I will still be OK because that right path is there for
me
and as long as I keep myself open, take time to go
inside
and be still quiet and listen to my heart and soul
and come out readied for attuned recognizing for
what will appear

and I may feel it like a warm uplift inside me
like the following of a Star in the night sky

that's lighting my way from the inside.
And it will feel like something has clicked and
my wheels have fallen into the tracks and I will
know.

And even if it doesn't happen like that
or at least right away, what would I really have lost
and how much did it cost me, really, to do a little

star wishing?

Today, I will TRUST and ACCEPT that

the UNIVERSE WILL COME THRU and SURPRISE ME with the MONEY that is needed because

It can and It will.

And I will finally get it that the Universe **actually** *is* on my side and Today, I will get rid of my

toxic old beliefs about money and
I will accept that I don't have
to **do** anything to be "good enough" to
have it because I have nothing to prove
and

no one deserves it more than
me
not the people who have it
or don't have it or were born into it
or won it or lost it all

and I will accept that I already deserve it
just because I am human and I am
loved
and chosen and good without even
trying or doing

anything

at all.

Today, I will let the SNOW START
MELTING and let the
BALLOONS GO where they
may

I tend to accumulate things hanging over me
like a snowball rolling
even though I have only good intentions

and they say that when I really love you
it won't matter if the roles of our relationships
change
or whether we're friends or lovers or husbands
or wives or children or co-workers

but I want an agenda and blue prints
and I want to be able to see who's playing
which position so I can understand the rules

and prepare my strategy
but then I miss out on the moment with you
here and now and I get tangled up in the
words or labels I put on you.

You see, the baggage and the snowball
can bind us to each other,
sometimes for better, sometimes for worse.

and sometimes it's worth hanging in
when you don't know
until you know

or we be haunted with questions,
lasting...

and if I suddenly met you on the street
and I had no snowball baggage attached to you,
would I even like you or you me?
two people standing on the street
each holding 99 red balloons with both hands
some of happiness, some of hurt
and all the ones in between

and if we both let go of all of our balloons
at the same time
would they all go up
or would some stay or
would some float up and away
and come back to find us
another day?

and what would it be like
to stand there across from each
other afterwards,

totally free.

Meditation for the
POWER STRUGGLE
of the DIVORCE OR BREAK-
UP...

(just the price for getting this person out of your life)

Sometimes, when you've been in conflict for so long
and the power struggle has gone on and on until
you feel like you can't take it anymore and the
details
 seem to have lost their meanings...

the objects we're both grabbing for and pulling at
in our tug of war and the blame and the calling
names
and the who gets the house and the children if there
are children
and the money and the being right which proves
I'm strong and you're wrong and I won

and you can't HURT ME.

And all of those skyrockets and heartbeats and
nights of passion
and bills and sweat and presents and laughters and
surprises
and being betrayed and baited and scared and
framed
and lied to and shut out and hidden and shut down
and hated and lied to and lied to and lied to

yet loved.

And now like a piece of you is missing…and these
pictures
are passing before your eyes like montages from a
dreamy TV show
until eventually, it just gets to be too much for One
and even though
they don't want to, someone decides to just **give** or
say "Uncle"
or just throw down the toys and walk away.

And at first, the walking doesn't feel good,
more like running so you won't see me cry or see
me being broken
into pieces at a time (and there will be tears),

but then an idea comes from somewhere…
from a friend or the sky or up from the ground or
from an intuition out of the air and you know:

"_You have to look at it differently_"

and you will have to choose to stay in' it
and stay in it this way forever or you have to choose
something else.

And it doesn't matter what has come and gone.
It wasn't really about any of this. And even if you
walked away
with nothing right now, conceded on every point
and lost it all, it would be worth it because

that was just the price…
the price for getting this person out of your Life

and that all of those things together and times
would have added up to this moment and now,
just like taking off an old coat overworn and letting it
fall
to the ground over a puddle for someone new to
overstep
while it concealed and protected the yet unrevealed
for
the next customer.

And you can finally **breathe**…
and you are finally off the hook and all the little
hooks
that came along with it all too

and it was just the price of
getting this person out of your life
and leading you into

yours.

Meditation for a FAMILY WITH A KID ON DRUGS:
(stalemate)

I remember the day that you met me, when you showed and hit the air. I thought, the world better watch out and I knew there never had been and never will be anyone just like you. That you were something special. I think back on that day and I wonder *where did I go wrong* and how did I let you go off the tracks?

And why won't you listen to me anymore?

And I'm so afraid that it's all my fault. And I'm afraid that you'll runaway and you won't come home.
And I'm terrified that you could end up living in the park or that someone evil could steal you away yet I'm afraid for you to come home too because maybe you'll steal from us or lie right to my face and sometimes I want to put you on the street when I try to get you help and you won't take it or try or go. And I'm afraid that if I let you fall you might not

get up and you might even die and the world could swallow you whole and I wouldn't be able to live with myself and I don't know if I could go on if living is without you.

And even though I know, at least on some level, that a lot of what's happening with you and us now has so much to do with me and the past but sometimes it's just too hard to look at. But I can't turn back time and you're almost a full grown person now

and it's time for you to **snap out of it** and "**just say 'NO'**" and grow up and leave the past behind. I know that I smoked too much pot in front of you and drank too much and the marriage failed and we put you in the middle like a chicken bone. And I know I wasn't there because I was working or because I was drunk or I was down at the bar or cheating with my mistress or working and working and working or even just at home and stoned in the house – there but not there – because it showed that I was more partial to your sister or brother or someone else in the house who was more trouble than you and having their turn in the barrel…

And I'm afraid that you're not as strong as the world is dangerous and won't do as I say and not as I do because it's for your own good and even if it's just because I'm your father and I said so and because it's my job and **because I love you**.

And I'll understand that to train my dog right, I'll have change me and adjust my behavior and my voice but I won't get it with you and I'll point my finger in desperation when you don't respond when I drop the can full of coins and I'm still unable to see what I need to see -- that it's as much about me. And I'll still carry that worst case scenario picture around in my head of you running away and living in the street or in that park or my not letting you back in because you won't stop and I'll wonder which one might kill or come to your senses first. And I'll pray inside — twisted up in knots debating and going back and forth about whether or not I should bring you a blanket when the night is cold or even just

a sandwich...

Today, I will let this moment be JUST
CALM
and not BEFORE THE
STORM –or-

Today, I will allow for the possibility that
**maybe it's just quiet, Not
too quiet**

---

the wires got crossed and many hearts
wound up installed with little bird brains of
not 'good or bad or better or best' but:

HOMING PIGEON ALWAYS GOES
HOME

and Familiar took precedence
and like magnets drawn back onto themselves

we learned to keep circling the Tower
because it had become safe…
Safe in the unsafe because at least then
we knew what to

expect.

And now when the quiet comes,
I may not think I can trust it. I may miss it
and let it pass me by because I'm too busy
planning where to bury my mines
or make sure that all my fronts are being monitored
at the same time in the war room
where I sleep.

And maybe I don't know how to do the emptiness
of the absence of drama, unable to realize the good
when it is good and to believe that sometimes
calm comes after the storm and not before.
And I may believe (subconsciously)
that at least if the disaster is timed,
I can have some control over it
and self-destruction is better than

no destruction at all.

And I will ask myself which came first,
the pigeon or the egg or the egg
or the home or the storm or the calm?

Maybe I wonder if I don't want you anymore
and the attraction is finally gone because
the drama came first
and took all the mirrors and smoke when it went
and without them maybe I can't see anything at
all…

And what would happen if I did outgrow
the you I thought you were and the me
I thought I was and the need for them both
 and the walls came down and we could live

life not during wartime?

is

today, I will be with **what is**
not how I wish it would be or could be
or was or how it should be.
and I will just

let it be...

and leave it alone and not try to change
it

and I will **observe**.

And I will stop waiting for you
so my life can resume
and I will ask myself why have I given
you

so much Power? and I will accept that
actions speak louder

and I can stop putting my life on hold,
waiting for the 'in-case' you might smile
or touch me or just come out and speak
the word
"No..."

like scraps for a dog.

And I will stop puzzling over the
question:
"Is shutting someone out an act of
aggression?"

and Today, I will live in the IS
in case those right tracks never come
and that switch is broken
and the end of the line is that
if you wanted it different it would be
different
and why is that so hard for me to
swallow?

and I keep looking for which way
is the right way out of the roundhouse
and we just keep going around in circles

riding the rails.

Today, I will take a

LONG HARD LOOK
at me NEXT TO YOU
(and the people I'm close to...)

Do I feel better about myself
when I am next to you

and if not
why do I have you in my life?

Let me count the number of ways
I have sold myself out to be able to
tolerate sitting next to your

disapproval

(whether it is real of imagined)

to stay with you and
to stand by you

and how have those ways hurt you?

And when we love each other
so much, why can't we just

LIVE IN PEACE?

Today, I will not live LIVE IN YOUR DOGHOUSE ANYMORE

Puppies are so cute that everybody
loves them
and we put them on display like that
doggie
in the window for sale. And some dogs
get all
the attention and get shown off and
groomed
and trained and treated like people or
maybe better.

But most puppies take a lot of energy…
a lot of energy we're not always
prepared to give

and they don't have batteries we can remove
or remote buttons to turn them down
and they can chew on everything in sight and
we can be disappointed in ourselves because we're
missing the secret of doing the just right thing
to get them to behave even though a puppy is
just a puppy and we're doing the best we can
in a naturally imperfect situation and

we say to ourselves
why didn't I see this coming?

And sometimes dogs bite
even when all they want is to be loved
even the hand that feeds...

and I get tired of begging for scraps

and I don't want you to put me down
or give me away to someone else
or worst of all put me in the car and
drive me out into the middle of nowhere,
open the door and dump me out,
just leave me there and just drive

away.

And today, I will accept that I no longer
have to live
in your dog house whether or you need
me to or not…

and you no longer have to live in mine
when we could run

in a pack of 2
like we used to

and when all I really want is to just lay
with you, in the sun

with my tongue hanging out
 on a hot day and maybe

chase a ball.

Today, I will get honest with myself about WHY I DON'T WANT TO GO HOME..?

or Meditation for a WORKAHOLIC

_____

If I told you I worked 7 days a week
what would you say?

Why do you need so much money?

You must be a very hard worker.
 - or -

Is there something you're running
  away from?

or

why don't you want to go home?

And when you do get home, you sit down
and get sucked into the TV like that little
blonde girl, Carol Anne in Poltergeist
who got trapped behind the glass in that
noisy snow

and I don't realize that I'm getting sucked
in too, sucked into my own rabbit hole of

Missing You,

the same one I've been down and used
a thousand times…before I even met you

using it to lose the me I think needs losing.

And so we're lost to each other and
to ourselves like leaving only empty shell outlines
of angels made by people who used to live here,
just imprints of who they were and
who they were supposed to be in that

other kind of snow.

Today, I will realize that

I CAN DO ALMOST ANYTHING
(if I think I can)…

We don't like Once Upon a Time.
I'm not very interested in where.
And there is a distance between I can do it
and I will do it and I made it.
And sometimes I may feel like it's too much
and I may get bored and discouraged inside of it
and I won't know that <u>I am supposed to</u>
<u>feel discouraged</u>
when I lose that shoe or get sick from eating
 some poison apple from someone who's against
me
or I get swindled out of the cow for some stupid
magic beans.

But I have to learn it somehow…that I am supposed
to self-doubt and that that's part of the homework.

Rome wasn't built in a day and that watched pot
never boils
and the medicine WILL GO DOWN with or without
a spoon full of sugar and even the Vampire
in Twilight
is going to burst into flames in the sun one day.

But slow but sure does win the race
and instant change may happen
with frogs made for kissing but in real life
there will be times when I have to tell myself
"I THINK I CAN, I THINK I CAN"
even when my wheels are grinding
on what feel like the wrong tracks and
I will want to give up when it doesn't happen
right away.

But on the other side, I will see that the destination
isn't really the destination and that much more
important is how I change and the expansion of
myself.

And I will become aware when the top of the hill

is in sight

— that hill I knew I couldn't climb —

that the journey is not about what happens to me
but what I do with it

and I will feel so different when I know
 on the other side that

I knew I could
I knew I could.

Today I will be grateful for

My STATE OF INDEPENDENCE

Freedom is one of those strange things.
Too much of it can hurt.
Not enough can suffocate you.
So one more time, you're looking for the Goldilocks effect
 and the just right.

And on most holidays all kinds of consciousness gunk
 gets stirred up about the past, present and our fears of the future.

And sometimes it feels like that
ain't my America and it's not the same for you and me

even though I like Little Pink Houses
and I want it to be. But

Baseball, hot dogs, apple pie and Chevrolet...

never were much my speed and I never really
wanted them to be.

But it still doesn't feel good to be left out
whether that's really happening or not
and there are many ways to be criminalized and
outlawed which we can get so easily attached to
and turn into a shield.

But the truth is it is not perfect here
and some people do have an unfair advantage
 but that's just the call of the wild.
Not everyone can play football or live
in Barbie's Dreamhouse (even though it is Pink).
And even though you can find hypocrisy all over this
land
and from sea to shining sea,
there is no country in the world doing it better
right now and this is THE BEST PLACE GOING
TO BE DIFFERENT,

broken as it is.

We live in the Nation of Change and Independence
isn't

something that lives in the soil or in the banks or on
the freeway.
True Independence is inside us and it's a state of
Mind
and theoretically, no one can take that from me
unless I give them the keys.

And even though sometimes I think it sucks here,
like when an election is stolen bold faced
in front of a whole world to see or a war is fought
over the false pretenses of a man who says
"nukUlar"
and whom we all "mis-underestimated" and who still
left that child behind,

I will choose My America – the New York
 that will be healed after 2 skyscrapers are raised
to the ground and an attempt to kill us
turns into a mushroom cloud of love in its wake
and a tree does still grow in Brooklyn.

And I'm just like that stupid girl in the forest
who was dumb enough to go into a house
where bears live.
All I can do is try to find my way.
And if I don't like my Pink House, I can move.
And if I don't, I must take responsibility for staying.
And if I decide instead that this is where I want to be
all I can do is the best I can do with my little piece
of the world and my square of the quilt

and do what I can to make it a better place
for You and Me and try to like Jackie DeShannon
said, put a little Love in Your Heart
and that's the best I can do
and the closest I will ever get to

just right

Today, I will accept that even though I love you and it causes me great Pain,

I WON'T GO DOWN WITH YOUR SHIP

Sometimes I love you so much, it feels like you're part of me.

And it is so hard to see you in pain and struggle but sometimes

I can feel like I can feel myself eroding. And I wish I had a pill

that could fix it or a special book or a therapist even a magic wand.

And stuck out here in the currents with no land in sight

I can see our ship is taking on water and I can see it

rising up above my feet, above my ankles, heading towards my

knees. And there will come a point soon when I will have to make a

decision.

And other people won't understand.

But I can't go down with you.

And it can be even more confusing

– when sometimes I too believe in the some things

Supernatural –

to hear you talking about spirits or other people

living in your same body or voices telling you what to do.

And it makes me feel like a bad Husband or Wife or

Mother or Father or friend to be floating out here

feeling like I've abandoned ship when I haven't even

walked the plank yet and without a life-preserver

and the last thing I would ever want to do is betray you.

So I will float here and stay close by

keeping my head above water as long as I can

because I think I might be able to save myself

but it's getting more and more clear that I can't save us both.

And as the waves bob me up and down like a doomed apple

at a child's Halloween party, and currents carry me,

I will pray – for you and for me and for us both –

because I don't know what else to do…

maybe pray for a storm or a wind of change

to somehow fix it all, to mend the hull of your broken

little brain that I'm afraid I'm the one who broke

and I will hang onto believing in the possibility because

I have no other choice but to hope for

Divine Intervention.

Today I will choose to **BELIEVE**
that **THERE IS A GOOD**
ENERGY
RUNNING THE UNIVERSE

and what if we could Imagine or even
just pretend for just one day we could know
100% that this were true?

Ask yourself, how would your life be different?
Yours, mine and ours?

And what if the Universe could save me
from my negative thinking if I asked it to
and I could realize that that Energy is my
only Source of Good and Happiness and that
no person, place, thing or situation...
no job, relationship or even family can be
all of that for me...

that these are only channels through which

It's/My greatness can reach me.

That I could know It is on my side and It wants
me to be Happy.

And maybe you could call it a Higher Power
or God or the Great Spirit or even just that
Big Positive Loving Intelligence?
And what if I didn't have to care less about
what anyone else called it or thought about it
and I wouldn't have to act as a recruiter
or try to prescribe anyone else's ideas or beliefs
and I could just let myself be myself?

And what if we could know that It would always
be on my side, standing behind me and backing me
up
and coaching me through my Intuition
from the inside out if I can learn to listen.
and that It's Power was Unlimited and it could do
anything and was helping me, even if I don't see
how yet and I could know that there is
nothing too Big or too Small.

And how would things be different if we just acted
in these ways even just for 24 hours?

How would people be different if they had a Spirituality
involved in their lives? And how would the

world change?

Today, I will **finally wise up** and get it
and remember that:

I don't take my toys
to people who
break them.

---

especially, if they've broken them
before.
And more than once before.

But then, hey

Better late than never.

And I will give myself a break and know that
I'm not the only one who has been a
selective slow learner in this department

And no matter how I may have paid for this
in the past, and even if it was dearly,
it's never too late to catch a tiger
by the toe and sometimes it's OK

that you can't win if I don't

let you play.

Today, I will LET MYSELF BE UNCOMFORTABLE
and I will turn in my TICKET
ON THE TERROR TRAIN

They say happiness can hit you like a train on a track

but I almost always have plenty of time to see it coming.

And the fear of the pain -

or the pain of being in fear of the pain we are afraid is coming –

is worse than the pain of

what actually happens when real the feelings arrive.

Like that train on a track

with a killer on the loose

running from car to car and hiding

in my shadows seeming further away

in the distance than it actually is

but turning out to be moving much faster

than it looks and fast enough to take you out

and take you by surprise.

And one more time, my perceptions

are off and objects in the rear view mirror may
appear closer than they are –

not further away – and I need to learn how

to turn my volume knob down.

I heard someone say:

 "I need to be in the problem otherwise I don't feel
like

I'm alive and I can't sit with the feelings when there
is no drama."

And we need to learn to get comfortable with

being uncomfortable because that's normal life.

And we no longer need to live like self-destruction

and the train won't really stop anyway

just like in the movies when Jamie Lee Curtis
pulls on the emergency cord and nothing happens.

Because usually there is no emergency…
and most of the time, I can see that that train wasn't
a locomotive but more like a little engine choo-choo
that thought it couldn't take it or thought it might die.
And maybe if I don't enough times,
I'll be able to smarten up and realize I could just
step off the tracks or maybe pay attention
to lights and flashing signs and just

not step onto them

in the first place.

Today, I will KNOW and STAY OUT OF MY OWN TRAPS

(or Anytime the Hunter gets Captured by the Hunter -or-
  Anytime the Game gets Captured by the Game...)

Once upon a time there were two people who met
walking down a road. They looked different and
they came
from different places but they found themselves
heading for
the same destination at the same time because they
needed
to fetch

a pail of water.

What they didn't know was that one of them needed to be
punished and rejected (so that he could be forgiven
so he could know he could be loved)

and the other one needed to be hurt and wronged
so she could shut out and shut down with reason
(so that she could know she could be safe and
protected from being used...)

and each thought the other was more to blame,
although they each knew they were a little at fault
too
but they each knew the other was really the
Predator
and the real cause of it all

that in fact, they had been tricked
and that while they were innocently on their merry
way
they had been unlucky and stepped into a snare
trap
that had been set by the other.

What they didn't see was that they both wanted the
same things.
To be protected and to be safe. To be forgiven
and loved
unconditionally. And they each just wanted to be
happy.

But that in trying to protect herself,
she had become the hunter
and the setter of her own trap and he
had done the same in forcing her to push him away.

And they had each laid their traps without knowing it
and although they were meant for the other,
they also fell in.

for if you set a trap, knowing or unknowing,
a foot will come...

even if it is your own

and then who will be the one responsible
and the one who suffers when you have to

chew it off, again?

Today, I will be EXCITED about GETTING BACK INTO LIFE

No matter how I may have been waylaid,
I will realize that these things have been brought to me

on purpose

and that everything I experience comes with a lesson
the Universe would have me learn about Life,
about what is really important and about

who I really am.

Even when I think I have lost hope
and whether it seems like my body,
my bank account, my family or even my Spirit
seem fractured. And I will be grateful
for having a family to stand by and support me.

And if I don't have one, I will create one
and even if I do have one I will create more of
one anyway.

And I will realize that I do not have to go it alone
and I can have the honor and the privilege of being
the one to stand by and stand next to and support
and be USEFUL if their hard times come.

And I will know that I am being guided and
delivered.
And I will remember that I have been through
hard hard times before and everytime, in the long
run,
they have only made me a stronger, wiser and a

better person.

Today, I will admit
I LOVE MY DARKNESS

We think that we have absolutely no control over
our feelings.
But while they may be unruly at times and they
sometimes
they may even seem to paralyze us,

this just isn't true.

There may be times when they take control of us
and those times may seem like they go on forever…
like in times of loss or sickness or when
the bottom falls out from under.

And we may even have problems with our emotional
biology.
But the idea that there is nothing we can do
about our negative feelings is a myth that we love
to spread like smoke over water.

But even in these cases, I still have many choices about
how I feel and how I choose to feel, and whether I am
prepared to fight or work or whether I even want to
or whether I want to just lay down and emotionally die
like an actress in a black and white movie from
the forties
dying of consumption.

No one trick is going to work for everyone
and there is no solution that's 'one size fits all.'
But there are also tools of destruction I can use
to make myself worse like addiction and
isolation and rage or self-pity.

But most down periods don't last forever.
And most up periods don't either.

But what if I imagine the possibility that even with
significant and consistent downs I can still have
an overall hopeful and positive life.

And sometimes I need to admit that it's easier
to live at the mercy of my feelings because
it's easier to have someone like a specter named
Feelings to blame and sometimes I need to admit
that I am being served by and I am attached to my
pain and my

darkness.

Today, I will think about

'WHAT WOULD I BE WITHOUT THE WORDS AROUND ME...?'

...the words that surround me

the letters before or after your name?
the titles, the praises, the convictions
the accusations and the accolades
the names you have been called and
the ones you have dished out
that all give you the illusion you know
who and what you are, good or bad.

And what would it be like to be free
of all those words, fencing you in
and trying to define you,

making you forget that you can never
be defined and that no matter what the words –
the ones being said or the ones that you are saying,
even the ones you are just thinking
or saying to yourself before or after
the ones that just came out of your mouth.

And today, I will remember that I am free…
beyond all words even the ones in the tattoos
down the arms of a convict that need to be
erased like regrets or the shiny words
on a sash that said Miss America or
Miss Venezuela…

that words can never be more than just letters
or symbols strung together, not even complete
ideas and they cannot make me us who we are
and that we are free and we can always redefine
and I can always

recreate myself.

Today, I will realize that

THE MAP IS NOT
THE TERRITORY
and
2 PEOPLE CANNOT
DRIVE ONE CAR
 at the same time

I don't need to know How.

And sometimes it's not my job
to figure it out. Sometimes I don't need
to know when or why or why not or where

but I can know like I know
I will eat turkey on a Thursday in November

and sometimes it's just my job to know
it will be figured out…
that it has already been figured out
that it has already been taken care of

to remember to breathe.

and I can get so lost just trying to read the map
that I forget

the MAP IS NOT THE TERRITORY
and two people can't be driving

one car
at the same time

Today, I will realize
MY WORDS HAVE POWER
and
I WILL SEE WHAT I AM DOING
TO MYSELF with them

If this is a WOES Contest, I can beat you

and if this is a woes contest,
I **will** win, even if I have everything.

Even If I'm more well off or well educated or
more well blessed
because I can store up woes in my mind
like a warehouse and they don't respect
any rules of relativity

and I can turn the closing of a freeway
into a threat to end civilization as we know it

or the murder of a little girl far away or
some dirty pictures some politician texted

– to someone probably not so innocent –

(because on some level
maybe he wanted to take himself down)

into what I think is something Real.

And I will forget that words are ideas
and I will convince myself that these words are
important
to me or they have something to do with me
as if they were here in the room with me right now
like a lottery ticket I'm actually hoping might win

and I won't see that most of my fears never come to
pass

and I can cast my words out like a fishing net
or a curse out into the future
and I won't see what I'm doing to myself or to you
and I won't even remember what I remembered
to forget…

to stop and ask myself that age old question:
"are you a good witch or a

bad witch?"

Today, I will ask you to just be
MY WITNESS and I will learn
to just be
YOUR WITNESS too

You can be talking to someone and
and in the middle of telling them something
they start telling you how you shouldn't feel

and they decide it's like a riddle
and they will solve it for you
to make you not uncomfortable
and save you from your difficult feelings
and without even knowing it
save themselves from being in the presence
of your difficult feelings because they are
becoming uncomfortable with them

all with nothing but
good intentions.

But why can't you just let me have the feeling
without thinking I am trying to predict the future
and when it's the holding them inside that
will keep me stuck?

And today, I will learn how to ask

"DO YOU WANT FEEDBACK ON THIS?'
when someone asks me to listen
and I will learn to speak up and ask for the same
when my turn comes and I will realize that
if someone cannot give me back the same
it doesn't mean it's my fault or they don't love me
but maybe they just don't have the skill or the
capacity.

I won't take it personally and I will let them just be
who they can be and I will learn to find someone
who can really listen the way I need and
I won't go back to an ear who has shown me
it can't give me what I need.

sometimes the most loving thing I can do is listen
and keep my mouth shut even if I don't agree with
what you're saying or how you're going through it

because sometimes I'm not even asking for your
compassion
and all I want is a witness to stand by me in my
process
and let me work it out

for myself.

Today, I will not TAKE THE POISON and WAIT FOR YOU TO DIE

Why is it we can be in a room of 100 people
and be surrounded 99 who love us and one
who doesn't… and then all my attention goes to that
one?
Why doesn't he like me? Why doesn't she like me?

Good supportive people in your life can be hard to
find
but I am so good at finding the sour apple in the
barrel
and biting into it and soaking in the bitter juice.

Is it just because I'm used to it or is it something I
need?

Or is just that I don't know how to spot unconditional love
because it's so foreign to me.

And if I came upon it by accident, would I know what to do
with it or would I discount it or brush if off instead of
letting it in and believing it's true?

Or would I do something to break it or destroy it
or sabotage it without even knowing that was my plan.

And I will ask myself whether I have been that bitter apple too
for someone else and where this crazy recipe came from
and why I am trying to bake this

PIE?

Today, I will try to find the balance between
TOO CLOSE AND TOO FAR

We think that if it isn't silhouettes against the sunset,
it isn't good enough. Or if we're part
of a single parent family that means we're less
and that when people divorce it's simply a failure.

And when it comes to too close or too far
in the real world,
it can be hard to find a balance.

They say that in love or romance more distance
is actually healthier. That we need to be two whole
people holding hands walking down the beach
together
rather than 2 halves trying make a whole.

But sometimes it can seem like you just get in the way
of my life or I'm getting in the way or yours
and the more I forget about you or even ignore you
the better we get along. That the more I learn
to live without you, the better it is for both of us

although the less of us there is.

Or we could do it the old way like
two leeches closed circle leeching off each other
and draining each other at the same time,
using each other to stay alive and in
complete sincerity
but still not being able to mistake the drama
and intensity for love without knowing something's
wrong
and just wondering "Why?"

So today, I will try to find a balance between too close
and too far even if I don't know what just right
should feel like or how I ended up in this forest
in this house with the three beds.

First in the one that was too small
and then the one that was too big
and still looking for the one that's just right.

And if we found it, would I be able

to tell?

Today, I will GET RIGHT with MYSELF

If you could watch yourself,
you would know.

If you could step outside yourself and see
what you were doing and who you were with
and who you cared about, you would see
that you are a better person than you think you are.

And if you could stand back and notice,
you would relax and so many of your own
judgments
about yourself would just drop away.

And if you could tap into the deeper parts of
yourself,
you would be amazed at the intelligence inside you
and the ability to know, and the answers and the
wisdom you are passing by

day by day by day by day.

And Today, I will understand that the ATM
is not my source and the family money tree
is not my source and having to go back to it
again and again is not my source and can't define
'who I am.' And your Opinion of me
is not my source or the good or the bad you have
done
and all the things you're not good enough at
or all the things you're not accomplishing
fast enough.

And I will get it that none of these can be
my Source or my Identity…that what I am
is beyond all these things.

So I better get right with Myself and the
Greatness within and beyond words
generating from inside me that is connected
to everyone and everything…
so I don't

waste anymore time.

Today, I will not try to decide whether
the change is good or bad.

  And I will wait to see when I get there.

I don't have a crystal ball but I try to read one.
I try to see even in my sleep.

And I'm not meteorologist.
I just have dreams about playing one on TV.
But I still try to forecast, trying to know
which way the wind will blow

and with every hour of fear I spend
of 'will there be thunder'
or 'will there be storms?'
or will there be calm

and which would be worse…
and if there were,
would there be anything left to say?

and I will say it out loud that
I have never been a blue calm sea
I have always been a storm.

And maybe I never did want to be...

And when the morning comes after...
and if I found a diamond in the rough
would I know what to do with it or
even know it for what it was before
it had been

cut.

Today, I will CLEAN OUT THE ROOM

they say that Love is like a hotel room
and no one new can check in until the people
in there before have checked out and the room
has been totally cleaned. And they say that energy
in our lives works the same way.

Until I have cleaned out the junk in the room of my life
that I'm still holding onto, the good that
I'm longing for can't move in and take over either.

But the Universe has plans and
Lessons will be learned either way and
sometimes I can't get in my own way even
if I want to and sometimes It can have a way
of working around me and moving
what needs to go out of my room without
my doing.

Even if It has to pull it out of my cold
dead hands.

And sometimes I can't tell if it's because
you won't go or because I won't let you leave.

And I can have all my bags packed and be ready
to go and find myself just standing here outside
your door and with the taxi waiting and blowing his
horn.

And I wonder how can it be that I haven't even left yet
but already I'm so lonesome I could cry.

And sometimes I don't want to say goodbye,
even if your name is sadness or regret or
living in the past and I know it
or even just a refusal to take a chance
on Life being good or the old Me
I don't know how to let go of before I can
find the new Me to grow into.

And part of saying hello is saying goodbye
so I can go

or I can just sit down here surrounded
by my baggage and miss my plane
and just tell myself that I can always catch the

next flight.

The Fairy Tale of the 9 Fingers
-or-

Today I will ask myself when is it okay to give up?

and how many times can you draw a line
 in the sand

and then step back and then step back again
only to draw another and another

You've got it the way you want it
But what about the hook on the other end of the
line?

And am I willing to accept things as they are
and would it be worth cutting off one finger

 if that's what it takes to save the other 9?

THE FAIRY TALE OF 9 FINGERS

And once upon a time there was a woman
who had been wronged very very badly
by her husband and it caused her great pain.
And as the punishment, in order to let him stay,
the woman called upon a local Witch who
cut off his finger and gave it to the woman
to put in a jar up and keep up on a shelf.

And the woman held it for ransom.

And the only thing the woman would say
was 'be patient, be patient" and she would
not give anymore.

Maybe she knew she might never give it back
or maybe she was waiting for something
or maybe she just didn't want to think about it
because just thinking about it hurt.

And she grew comfortable living in passive control
that was keeping her safe. And she would never

admit it but it was working for her with things just
that way.
And for now, that was just the way she wanted it.

And in time, the finger on the shelf in the jar
turned into a heart of lust and the heart of lust
turned into a heart full of pain and then
the husband's
9 remaining fingers began to fall off all on their own
one by one and with no cutting.

And all the wife still said was
'be patient, be patient…'

And how could it have been really been
in her interest to give the finger back for she had
learned
to take care of her needs alone and she had learned
not to need the man and even to do better on her own.
And for the first time in her life, she could make sure
that she could be safe and no one could ever

hurt her again.

Until the heart in the jar finally turned
from pain to dust and as the man lay dying
he asked out loud "Why didn't you just take the

other 9

in the first place?"

Today, I remember that
I DON'T NEED TO KNOW
THE HOW

How many things have happened in my life
that I thought would be **impossible?**

Today, I will sit and think back and try to count them.
And I will see that figuring out the How is not my
job.

How many things did I think I could never
bounce back from or how many false moves
did I make that turned out to be corrected and then
turned out to be all right and even

for the good.

The truth is that the Impossible happens.
It's happening in your Life right now

and although dodging the bullet doesn't mean
it wasn't shot, when we are willing to live rightly
and just do the best we can do —
next thoughtful action by next thoughtful action, —

we can get through almost anything.

When I can know the destination and
turn it over and let the yellow bricks
lay themselves out before me
I still get where I was needing and usually hoping
to go in the first place unless there's
something better. And

THE WAY WILL BE MADE.

Today, I will ask 'WHO WOULD I BE IF I LOST EVERYTHING?"

They say that love is a dangerous game to play
and that trust is fragile but what made it special
made it dangerous

that these could take you to the top
of the mountain or into the stars or leave you
broken, even if you just stood by like a witness
not speaking up but just letting your life
happen to you instead of saying

'No.'

And how much could you get for your soul
and what could make you sell yourself out?

How much would you be willing to pay
if you had seen it clearly or how much
would you be willing to gamble now
if it were a game?

And how could you end up needing so much
anyway?

And sitting in a house surrounded by all
of the things we've tried to add to "Me"
and in a life surrounded by the people
who make me think I know who I am,

today I will ask myself what would I be
without anything? ALL OF IT…

what would I be worth if it were all
just stripped away leaving me just
with me and I had to be just who I am?

and if you had to start all over,
would you testify or just go quietly
into the silence of your own emotional

WITNESS PROTECTION PROGRAM.

Today, I will realize that

if I am angry with you
or if I am wanting something
from you

　too much

I am believing and investing in
my own

　incompleteness.

Today, I will know that SQUARE BY SQUARE, I will be SHOWN the way

I can feel afraid when I step out of my box
or I go out of my circle of safety

whether my comfort zone is never driving
outside of my little town or jet setting week to week
on business or in glamorous circles around the
world

without ever
  touching down.

Living in my circles, I know what to expect
and I can think I am protected
but to move forward, I MUST dip my
foot in the pool.

But I can know
when I am attuned
that I will be caught even if I fall.

Sometimes I need to take chances
to know that I'm alive and
I can know the other end of the checkerboard
that I'm playing to and even see
that I'm able to be there and myself doing it
but not know how to jump

but if I know in surety that the way will be made,

the road is already paved.

Today, I will trust that

THE ROAD KNOWS
WHERE I NEED TO GO

I can choose to turn this
into a trauma or a tragedy
or an emergency

or I can choose
to let this be no more than a

blip

on the screen of my Life.
But I have a choice.

The Road knows where to take me

like the flower that contains its own
blueprint
for how it is meant to unfold
and doesn't need to be told how to grow

and the Road doesn't need to be told
where to

go.

Today, I will recognize that my Life is a SYSTEM

In Chinese medicine they say "where the good Qi is weak

the bad Qi attacks" and that the body is a whole system and

not just isolated parts.

And I will realize that today is not only just one day but one of a system of many days that make up my lifetime.

And even though I need to stay in this day because it is the only access point I can have to the energy of the divine, no one day can be the make or break point of my Life. Even if it's my wedding day,

my graduation day, my day in court or even
the day that I am going to die.

Today, although I will stay in the moment,
I will realize that even if "The Day" I'm dreading or
wishing for comes, it is but one more day, one piece
of a greater whole and that there were many
yesterdays that lead up to this moment and
there will be

tomorrows.

Today, I will look for the LIGHT INSIDE ME

There is Light inside every one of us.
We may not know it but it is still there.

Like in the moment when we see our
new child
for the first time or in the moment when
we
love our dog or when an old friend
moves away or when we are reaching
our

highest potential.

And some people believe that the same
Light
inside of you is the same light that
expands
inside of me, that there is only ONE light
and we are all connected.

Who can say for sure but
wouldn't it be nice?

And today, I will look for and be aware of
ANY Light inside of you and me
instead of expecting and finding a world
of

darkness.

Today, I will realize that I AM THE TEACHER

_____

and that I am teaching everyone around me
with my words but even more in the actions
I take and how **I walk.**

And I am teaching and re-teaching myself
about what the world is and about
the nature of people and

who and what I am.

And you are the teacher too
and every one of us is
even if we don't realize.
And you never know what someone is
learning or picking up from you.

And we are all gifted with this great
privilege, honor and responsibility
although we rarely pay attention to it
aside from a small number of words
that come out of our

mouths.

Today, I will know I don't need to
SWEAT THE DETAILS

Your new Life is already here even if you
don't see it all the way yet.
Don't turn away from your future and try
to hold on to or look back on the past.

Backwards wishing never got you anything
before and now that the chips are down
it's an even worse time for it now.

I have some things to tell you that could
become secrets if they remained untold.
And we all know how keeping secrets is still

a recipe for disaster inside.

And we have choices to react or respond
to what happens in our lives, even the mistakes
we've made.

But there is no hole inside me that some
outside something will complete or fill up or fix.
There never was a pothole in the first place.
And It's no good to overneed anything...
even when it's something good for you
if you think you need it to make you know

who you are.

The everything I need answer
that was inside me before and all along
is still inside me now

and today, I will visualize it
and I will know where I'm going
and I will know that it's still already
taken care of

and I won't sweat

the details.

Today, I will face the TURNING POINTS of my Life

There comes a moment
when the arm slams down
and the click of the chain catches
and it starts pulling forward
the cars of the little train.
And there is no

turning back.

And all you can do is hold on
until it's over and your
life is like an image of a
roller coaster

and everything rises
until that moment of intensity

and the tiny chance that even though
it's impossible, you might
fly off the tracks this high and plummet
to your

final destination.

Until the car jerks to a stop
snapping you back against
the back of the seat and the
reality of normal life and into the quiet
of the brakes, like pistons, exhaling.

And there is this moment
and there are the events leading
up to this moment and your life is like
before and after,
like a turning point
and for better or worse
there is no going backwards
because this train

only goes in

one direction.

Today, I will see my FEARS are LIKE HOLOGRAMS

---

 and today, I will know that they are not real.
And I will walk through the holograms of my
fear like apparitions in a

Haunted Mansion.

Like ghosts of self-doubt and limitation
and a world I see as against me.

And I will let myself be comforted by the
strongest part of me, my Highest Self
which knows there is little difference
between us except for a few minor adjustments
that can make all the difference.

And no matter how scared I feel or how
the night terrors…or how loud the wind blows
I will keep going and I will be strong
even if I can't sleep

and no matter what it feels like is hiding
under the bed, even when I know
there is nothing there,

I will stay **in my own bed**
and I will make it through the whole night
and find the strength to comfort myself
even if I need to cry

and I will realize that the only holograms
and monsters there ever were

were **projecting**

from inside of me.

Today, I will know that when the
STORM is too much, I can PULL OVER and WAIT IT OUT.

Sometimes, we have to tell ourselves
that things are going to work out

and sometimes you have to tell yourself
things are going to turn around
until Life catches up and they do.

Like when you can't see the way when you're driving
in fog or heavy rain and you can't see where
you're going except for what's right in front of you
in the headlights.

But if I'm careful and I go slowly
I can still keep going though I may even have to
pull to side of the road to rest or give up or call for

help.

And even if it feels hopeless, we can remember that
a homing pigeon can find it's way home even after
600 miles

and if I get waylaid or lost,
the storm will pass and I will be
back on the road in time.

And I can know that no matter how broken I feel,
I can wait it out until

the passing.

Today, I will remember that the MIRACLE IS IN PROCESS

Sometimes, I feel like if you left,
I wouldn't be able to take it
or if we parted...

And sometimes I feel like it would be a great relief
not to be fighting what can feel like a losing battle
 - off and on -
and running up that hill and wishing
we could be on the same side.

And today, I will realize that Forgiveness means
releasing or Letting Go not just the things
you're worrying about or pining over or the things
I'm threatened with losing

but also releasing or Letting Go of the things
I think are good in my Life that
I'm afraid I can't BE without or I think
I have to have to be Happy.

And being willing to live and be OK without them
because I don't know.

And today, I will remember that Miracles have
happened to me before and though it may be
impossible to see in this moment, they are

in process

right now.

Today, I will WALK TALL AND GO WHERE THE LOVE IS

Sometimes it feels like the world is falling down
around you.

Like you've lost your house and your wife
is leaving you and your dog is sick
and you've ended up in the

mental hospital.

And sometimes it feels like your life just couldn't get
any worse.

But even in these moments, if you can see them,
there are occasions of beauty all around you.
And you can remember that most of the moments
in your life are not like this.

And you will be loved again and you are
already being loved right now.

Maybe you end up having a great roommate in the mental hospital? Or maybe you end up stumbling across
answers where you didn't even know you had questions
and you identify the blocks that have been keeping you stuck
and walking in circles.

And then maybe Life takes your Life into another direction
where you didn't know you were supposed to go
and choosing that different road makes all the difference.

And I will get through the hard times either way.

And back out in the world, I will be careful about the people
I choose to have around me and who I walk with because
they can either lift me up or bring me down and I will only

WALK TALL AND GO WHERE THE LOVE IS.

Today, I will PICK UP THE PIECES OF ME

It's funny how easy it is to throw away
something you never earned.

And funny the pieces of me that I discarded on the
way down
so that I could love you while trying to get you to
love me.
And trying to get you to stay and approve by

editing who I was.

Like an addict craving for alcohol or sex or food,
that craving for love is never just a craving
but a distortion and a distraction from the
unpleasant reality of my life that I don't want to feel.
Like fertile ground already turned for planting,
just waiting for the seed to hit the earth that
couldn't be blamed on you.

And I'm sorry for the times you don't like me.
But I'm sorrier for the times I sold myself out
and then tried to lay it on you. And I'm sorry
for the times of those when I bought in and
believed you.

And who knew that holding onto me might mean
letting go of you…And today, I won't ask permission
and I will

pick up the pieces.

Today, I will not PROJECT

_____

And today, I will be here NOW
and I will remember that 1 day, 1 week, 2 weeks
is an eternity away,
as far away as
a hundred years

and in between, ANYTHING could happen,
even the unforeseeable, the unknown
and sometimes even

the impossible.

And I will remember that whatever I think
is happening right now or whatever illusion
I think I am seeing is only

a thought.

And I can choose to think it differently.
And I will pare away everything unnecessary
that doesn't really exist and all the
ghost stories I'm casting out into the future.

And I will remember what Ekhart Tolle said
and I will be here in the Power of the Now
and the stillness of completely letting go
into the silence of the present instant
where nothing else exists but

"No thought.
No problem."

(Part 1) Today, I will accept that SOME THINGS ABOUT ME MAY NEVER CHANGE

Today, I will realize that there may be some things about me that I don't like and some things about me that even cause me pain

that may never change…

and I will have to do the best I can to accept myself

as I am because some character defects may not be
removed and may seem so hard to get rid of

and so I may need to tailor my
life accordingly.

(part 2) Today, I will let myself be ONLY HUMAN

And when you have forgiven yourself,
it doesn't matter what you've done
if you have done the best that you can
do
and everything you can
to make things right. Because all you
can do
is the best that you can do.

And you can't do anymore than that.

People make mistakes and we are all
only human.

And so my problem becomes not that
the world
will reject me or not forgive me
for who I am and what I've done
but why I won't forgive myself.

But when I do, that's when life will
change
and flow in around me
and I will no longer be blocking
and keeping away the approval of Life's
embrace.

And today, I will just let myself be

ONLY HUMAN.

Today, I will let the BEST I CAN DO
BE GOOD ENOUGH

It's OK if you don't like me because
if I know I have done everything I can do
to be the best me I can be, then there's
nothing else I can do.

So if you don't like that, I'm sorry
and if you can't accept me as I am after that
then you always have the option to mosey.
Because when I have done everything
I can do to be the best me I can be,

I get to like me.

I am having a positive effect on people
and in the world and if you can't see that
or that doesn't mean anything to you, then

Oh well...

there's nothing I can do about it.

And I will realize that today, you are
going through a whole other trip of your own
through this whole thing we call Life
I can let what's yours be yours

and when I can know that I am doing everything
I can do to be the best me I can be,
then I can release anyone else's negative

opinions about me and just

let it go.

Today, I will recognize that NO
MATTER HOW MUCH I THINK I CAN
UNDERSTAND SOMEONE ELSE, I CAN NEVER
KNOW WHAT IT'S LIKE TO WALK
IN ANOTHER PERSON'S
SHOES.

We can think we can know someone.
Even someone we know very very well.
Even someone who is family or we think of as
family.

But there are things we will never know.
Even when they've told us the stories and
even when we know many of the facts.
We can't know the experience of where they came
from
or the memories that come along with that or how
it shaped them from the inside out or
what they're still carrying.
Or why they are the way they are.

And especially in conflict, it's important to remember
this and take it into account and try not to react
to just their surfaces and only what's showing up
in front of us in the present, not understanding that
our past is speaking through both of us right here,
right now.
And they may only know my surfaces too.

And this is not to make excuses or let
someone walk on me or be inappropriate with me
but so that I don't take on and take personally
what isn't really mine and make it all about me
when it's probably not about me at all.

And today, I will remember that no matter how you
appear,
everybody's got a

story to tell.

Today, I will realize that MY SAFETY CAN ONLY ORIGINATE FROM INSIDE OF ME
and I can find the SAFE PLACE inside of me
and when I need to, I can go there.

Sometimes, it can feel like your life is running into a brick wall.

Like a freight train and a damsel in distress tied down to the tracks.
Or a car on the freeway blowing out all 4 tires at once
when you never even got the

spare fixed last time…

But love means providing a safe place to retreat
from the world when everything goes to wrong.
Or having someone provide that safe space for you.

Or knowing that even if there is no one beside you
right now, you can provide that place for yourself.

Because my safety can only originate from inside
me
and you are the only one who can give it to you.
And you have the power to remember that safe
place
inside and out. And I can carry it with me
wherever I go and when I need to, I can
close my eyes and go there…
even if it's only for a few moments.

And if you're not already whole, nobody else
has the power to fill in the

missing pieces.

Today, I will accept my own INNOCENCE

and today, I will allow myself to be forgiven by forgiving myself and by forgiving you and releasing us both. Because I'm done serving your sentence and I'm done doing my time.

And I will be grateful that I am no longer living the life of a double agent or some kind of international 'spy who loved me' and grateful that I have paid my debts to society and I've been set free by a jury of my peers...

no matter who wants to hold onto sitting in judgment of me. And I have the profound desire to do whatever it takes to get through this period of my life and get this lesson and get on with the rest and let it be beautiful.

And no matter how afraid I am, I will see that
there is no executioner and if there were one,
the only person it could be would be me.
And I will have to stop sitting in judgement
of myself.

And no matter how many times I have been told
that life has to be hard and sad and a struggle,
I will let my mind, my attitude and my emotions be
healed.

And whether I was convicted, just on probation
or on parole, today I will discharge my number,
no matter how it looks on the outside and I will
confess to myself and let myself walk out a free
man and accept that I am

no longer living a

LIFE OF CRIME.

Today, I will understand that FORGIVENESS and SELF-FORGIVENESS ARE INTERTWINED

and you can't have one without the other.

And that forgiveness means accepting you
right where you're at considering everything
you've been through and where you come from.

That I see that you did the best you could do.

And that when all is taken into account, anyone
who had been through the same would have made
the same choices and that on some level,
no other choices could have been made or
were even possible.

And a person can't do more than they can do.

And I can see and know that the same is true for
me.
And that doesn't mean that I need to choose to stay
next to you...or that I need to go,
although I may.

But it does mean that I get to let go wherever
my physical body stands. And when I can see that,
then I can truly start to be able to forgive you

and forgive me

and set us both

free.

Today, I will understand that WITHIN EVERY GOOD BYE IS A NEW HELLO

Leaving can be difficult.
When you're in a bad place, it can be easier.
But more often than not it's difficult because
there are people you've become attached to
and because there are at least some good people
everywhere you go…

And it can very be tough to say good bye to even
awful people in our lives because we can get
used to them and even awful people have
silver linings
and even the negative familiar can get to feel
like home eventually.

And sometimes we let good byes drag on
because we don't know where we're going to
or the things that life will be showing you.

People die or leave us or sometimes we leave them
and that's just a part of the nature of Life

even when we didn't do something wrong.

But so often we can't see that within every good bye
is a new hello and that I have to clear out the old
to make the space ready for the new.
And sometimes the Universe pushes us out
of the nest before we think we're ready because
we can't seem able to make the leap on our own.

And if we tried to count the number of good bye's
we've had to live through and all the good bye's
I've had to say, would I also realize all of the
openings
they prepared for me and the new adventures
and the new spaces opened up for my Life
to flow into?

And maybe I just didn't know yet that there was
 someplace else

we had to GO.

Today, I will actually
LET TODAY BE
THE FIRST DAY OF
THE REST OF MY LIFE

because it's going to be anyway
whether I am aware of it or not.

And I will see that I have a choice about
what to expect and what to fear and to
understand that so much of our lives is
made up of interpretations or doubts.

And I can recognize that there will be opportunities
for me to count and reasons to stew in my
own gloom
and I have a choice about which ones to pick up
and take along with me and which ones to just
let drop because I just don't have the time
to be weighed down and I

haven't got time for the pain…

even by an illness or the loss of a job or
constant warnings coming through the TV
or by a natural disaster like a hurricane
or even the loss of a loved one because

the UNIVERSE NEEDS ME

And I WILL GO ON.

And unexpected good things will happen
to me today and they may be Big.

And I can choose to do my best to make more
happen even when it's a struggle to see through
the lightlessness that seems to be
in front of me right now.

And today, I will see that whatever happens
is a chance and a choice for me to make
something good out of it or to let it
pull me under.

And I will see that today and every day
is an opportunity to start over or simply
continue to move

in the right direction

Today, I will GET RIGHT BACK ON THE BEAM

Today, I will know that if I fall off
or I get off track or lose my balance,
I forget that I will be able
to get back on.

And it's hard to remember
that you could ever get back up again
especially when everyone in the
auditorium
sees and I forget to remember that maybe
this could be just a practice and maybe
there might not be judges scoring me
here today.
and just maybe it isn't really

the big Day.

But what I see is that because this isn't
part of the map I had mapped out
and because of the way my head talks
to me,
it's hard to remember to forget
when what isn't perfect comes along

yet it's so easy to forget to remember
that most things in this world

right themselves.

Today, I will not play the game called 'WHO IS MORE DAMAGED?'

You may think you are seeing someone who won't touch you.
And you may think you are seeing someone who won't talk to you.

But what you're really seeing is someone who can't be close.
Someone who is broken like you.

And it has nothing to do with me and whether or not I am wonderful. And why am I so easily convinced in selling myself out?

And there is a difference between someone
who won't be close to you and someone
who can't be close to you,
even though from the outside
it can be hard to tell the difference,

like maybe you never could tell unless
you had previously trained eyes.

And if I could realize and swallow that,
looking backwards,
it would explain so many things…

like all the bottles and promises and lies
and cold shoulders and cheats and
shut outs and shut downs and bodies
and videos and ragings and silences
and worries

like tennis balls passing back and forth
over a net made of nothing more than
strings and holes.

And why are people are so ready to tell us
what we want to hear when we pick teams
and point and say the other one's sicker
even though no one stood up and said
out loud that this had even become a contest?

and when there's more than plenty of sick here
– on both sides – to go around?
Whether everybody's

seeing it or not.

Today, I will get it that
LOVE IS LIKE A MIRROR

and you get back what you're giving
all the time including a level of love
when it's conditional.

And the Universe isn't stupid
and it's always paying attention
so you shouldn't expect anything more
or less.

And real Love doesn't not say

"I love you but here are my conditions.."

And Love is supposed to say "I will accept you
just the way you are." And even with all your
faults.

And if I ask myself whether I am ready to say
the words and how can I when there really are
things
about you that are unacceptable to me?

And how can I expect the same from you
when I know you have your own list that
you can hold up in the mirror for me at any time...

And today, I will make a list of all of the things

about you that I want changed and I will ask myself
whether there are any things on my list of changes
that I can drop or do without and what am I doing
here if I can't let them go?

And when will I get that when I make anything
about you too important, I am affirming my belief
in my own lack and need and incompleteness.

And when I am triggered by you, will I remember
to say "this is not about you" and recognize that
it's really about me and my belief in

my own imagined

empty spaces?

Today, I will MAKE A SPACE FOR THE NEW TO COME IN...

even though it sounds silly to me and
I will go ahead and do what everybody says.

And I will throw out with the old and clear a space
for the new to come in

even though it seems like there's no real reason
that it should make any difference.

And I will throw out old papers that I don't need
anymore
and I will give away the books I haven't touched for
years,
even the one's I never cracked open that still look
good
on the shelf.

And I will admit that it's time to lose all of these
things

and more that I've been carrying on my back,
just waiting for the right moment to come along
with that perfect purpose or that time to take down
for that that exactly needed fact or answer.

And I will be surprised at how this works every time,
without fail, and how throwing old papers and books
and trinkets away can pave the way for changes to
happen and come just because I'm not carrying
them

around with me anymore like ornaments on a
Christmas tree laid down to the ground after
New Year's Day has passed.

And I will be clear and aware and in readiness
to recognize the new energy's flow in of my

new life.

Today, I will remember that my ONE PURPOSE is to LOVE THE WORLD and the PEOPLE IN IT…

And I will focus on Giving and not
Getting and I will let Life take care of the rest.

Not for what I can get out of you or
what I can get out of the situation
or what I can get you to do for me

or how I can get you to owe me or
love me or sleep with me
or marry me or hire me
or give me what I want

or get you to leave me if it's too hard
to be close…

Like Money or a New Car or a chance
to trade for what's behind door #3
or to make it all the way to the end
of the show and the Showcase Showdown.

And I will remember that any good
that is ever going to come to me
will only come or stay if I am trying to do it

the right way.

And I will try not to forget this
5 minutes from now
or after my 15 minutes of fame.

And I will remember that when I don't live this,
things go very very wrong and all the things
on my list seem to crumble away like so many
pieces of blue cheese on a salad that was
just sad enough to begin with.

And even when I think you don't love me
and I get that twinge, I will remind myself
and be aware that I'm just feeling my
internal alarm clock reminding me to come back
to myself and telling me

I'm not right with myself.

Because if I really accept myself as I am,
I don't care so much if you don't like me,

although it's nice if you do –
and the crumbles become far less important
than they seemed.

But it's more important that I like me
than it is that you might disapprove
because I'm living to love you but
I'm not living for you.
And there's a big difference.

So I won't base my life on or live
according to your or anyone else's barometer
even if there's a dark drop in low pressure .
And I will give what I can, when I can,
but I will let nothing take away from me
and I will stay out of the results and stop living in
forecasts of a

slight chance of storms.

Today, I will
HOLD ON LOOSELY

The energy that created me
is what I am.

It's what I'm made of and It's the only thing
I can ever be. And the words I put it on it
don't matter because it's the same either way.

And whatever outside things I think I need,
I cannot be less without them – all those things
I think I need to add to me.

And there is nothing that can be taken away
from me and nothing that can make me more
whole or complete because I already am.

And when I realize this and let go and
even just

pretend

that I don't need whatever it is
and get myself to release,
then I can start to see that I really don't need
any of these things and then maybe,

just maybe,
what I was longing for

can find its way

into my hands.

Today, I will ask myself WHETHER I AM A SAFE PERSON?

There is someone who does not feel safe with you

It might be someone important or close to you or
It could be outside people who are less important.

Even if you don't think you're unsafe and it's hard
for you
to believe or you can't see how they could
see you that way. But sometimes we don't see
ourselves
clearly. And sometimes we can be completely
unaware of our impact on other people.

And maybe they're so scared that they can't come
out
and say it and even though they love you,

a piece of them trembles inside because of what
you
might say or how you might say it or how you
might react.

And they might even be afraid you could attack
them
if you told - even if not physically.

And there may be people who scare you too or
people
you don't feel safe around. And maybe you don't
let them know either.

But sometimes what I think doesn't much matter
and my actions speak louder
and my intentions
don't matter as much as my impact on you
and how you are receiving me.

Even when your ear hears out of proportion
and I think it's your fault.

And maybe I want to make the changes and
maybe I don't but if two people are going to work
things out
AT LEAST ONE OF THEM has to admit that
something's
not working and start making action changes
so that things either start falling into place or they
don't.

But either way, things start to come clearer.

And you may ask yourself...

"...this is not my beautiful house
this is not my beautiful wife
how did I get here...?"

And you may say to yourself

"...My God. What have I done?"

And maybe I can admit that
—at least for the moment —
I have decided to just SETTLE
and even if it won't be permanent

as you're letting the days go by
into the blue again...

and I'm not ready to burn down the house
and maybe, just for these in between days,

"settle" is not such a dirty word
and without any judgments, if
it's really just

just what's happening.

Today, I will decide to
TURN IT AROUND

_____

There is a difference between I want to have sex
and I want to have sex with you.

And there is a difference between
I want to be married and I still want to
be married to you.

And there is a difference between wanting
and not knowing whether it's possible
to be with you anymore and not understanding
how life changed.

It can be so hard to reconcile the differences
between
the life we were expecting and the one that actually
showed up and how all these things can turn out to
seem like

more than you bargained for.

And sometimes it's so hard to get ourselves to swallow
the truth of all this in the moments when it seems too much.

And I can bemoan and mourn or I can see the problem
of this moment as an opportunity to go INTO THE NOW
and juice the life out of it and re-make what seems like
the problem and embrace it and be grateful for even what I think is a devastation.

And there is always a lining and I have a choice
about whether or not to find it and
what to do with every situation.

And I can say thank you for this problem
and I can always choose
to see this as an opportunity to become stronger,
to become richer and learn more who I am
and what I'm capable of doing, accomplishing and being and feeling.

We can become free and even though
it's not visible in the middle.

And even when I think I can't bear it,
there is always a way to

turn it around.

Today, I will let it be OK to FEEL GOOD ABOUT THE CHANGES I HAVE MADE

———

…and to recognize that I have learned
some from the mistakes of the past
and learned to have compassion
for the people around me,

even when their actions are sideways —

 passive and aggressive.

And to learn to see through the
surfaces and recognize that it's not that
they're doing it "to me" or "at me" but that
they're just doing it…

and doing the best they can.

That many times what I'm seeing isn't rooted
in the right now but in a history of pain
that's manifesting in whatever the shape is
in front of me,

appearing in disguise and
afraid to show its true face.

And that even if someone can't see
the changes you've made, you don't
have to take it on because who you are

is changeless.

And shedding your old life
like a dried flaky skin that just doesn't fit anymore
that's been doing nothing but holding you back,
even when you're afraid to see that
your new healthier one has already begun...
in case a shoe the size of a house might drop
down on you

  right out of the sky.

And to have the

  guts to keep making the changes
still coming even when sometimes you are

  still afraid.

Today, I will see ONLY THE GOOD IN THE PEOPLE I AM CLOSEST TO

…and the people with whom I have the most important relationships in my life.

And I will see through the noise
of what appears to be important conflict
to what is really important beyond.

And I will identify any unfinished business
between us that I need to take care of
and I will do what I can do to make things

the best that can be now.

And I will make a plan with wise advisors
and I will remember that our Higher selves,

past the noise of the everyday conflicts
that seem so important, are the only
identities that really matter and that nothing
else is even really happening because

it's not what we will remember.

And I will choose to forget
all the rest that I may enjoy them
as much as I can before it's too late.

And I will let myself imagine what it would be like
for me if they were gone that we can be free
and happy together and

here.

Today, I will ask myself

WHEN I AM AROUND YOU, DO I FEEL BETTER ABOUT MYSELF...

or do I feel worse?

And if I feel worse, I will ask myself

What do I think that love is?

And why am I doing this to myself?

And what am I waiting for?

And I will ask myself, what would it take to

get me to stop

CHASING you

and when would I be ready to

GIVE UP THE GHOST?

Today, I will remember that this moment will not last forever

And that Life is like a giant cosmic library
and you can borrow so many wonderful things
but they all have a due date when they have to be
returned and no experience can belong to us
anymore than just on loan.

And all you can get to permanently keep
and take away is what you learned and the
memory of the experience.

And I will let this give me hope for positive change
when I cannot see the possibility of it
when you're not doing what I want
and Life's not giving me what I think I need.

Because the past is past and the time
has already been served and there is no longer

any guilt that hasn't been wiped away
and the nature of this world is change.

And I will no longer wait for you to give me time
off for good behavior or a someday to come
when you will stop being angry at me or
set me free.

And I will know that I could be unleashed
like Carrie after they dumped the bucket of blood
on her with all of that Power I never knew
I had inside me but none of the

rage.

Today, I will learn HOW TO NOT GET MY WAY part 2

And I will realize that when I don't,
even when it's something big,
it does not have to be a major calamity
and it doesn't necessarily mean that

my life is over.

Even when it's what feels like a
monstrous problem in the moment
like the loss of a job or a divorce or even
a serious illness.

It ain't over til it's over and any situation
I am in can turn on a dime –

in any direction.

And maybe we could try to let the Universe
design and shape the direction of my life
and let it tell me what to do and where to go.

And maybe something bigger could know
better than me…

And maybe I could learn to transcend
what seems to be so tragic now
until I can release it and let myself
be taken where it is I really need

to GO.

And how often has it turned out that what
seemed so awful Now was hiding a miracle
that only showed itself in the

long run.

I will ask myself... What am I holding back

from God today?

or from the Greater Energy or the Spiritual Flow
or your Higher Power or whatever the words are
for whatever it is that you've even just wondered
about
existing or not existing.

And what is so important that I am so afraid
will not be taken care of without me,
that will be dropped and lost as my world crumbles
and falls apart.

And today, I will ask if it's just possible
that the world in all its turnings might
do better without my helpful strategies
and if I just try to relax and figure out

what is my part to do as it shows up
in front of me, then what might happen...?

and what if I could hand over even the emergencies

to simply the way that things have
of working themselves out or falling
into place for better or even what initially seems

for the worse

until it turns

back around.

Today, I will give up all thoughts of WINNING

as if life were but a race or a game
or a contest or a marathon or a
Quiz show where I had to eat up
everything and paste whatever
I could get my hands on onto me
to make me have some kind of
value and meaning.

And I will imagine what it would be like
if there were no good and bad or
right or wrong and how that would
make me feel so relaxed in
being able to let go and realize
it would also mean there would be

No losing.

Even losing the people like you
I want to hang onto so much,

gone so shrunken like just like
a spec of dust.

And how could there be no losing
if they say one way or another
each of us is going to go away
unless there is a somehow we can't
confirm where everyone will actually
come back together and we will have

never really
been parted at all.

Today, I will realize that

THIS IS NOT SOMETHING THAT

JUST HAPPENED TO ME

while I sat innocently by.

And I will think about where I am and the negative pieces of my life and I will realize that while I am not completely responsible for the way my life is,

I had a hand

in creating the situation.

And I am not just a victim of

arbitrary winds.

Today, I will know that I have choices

even if they haven't been shown yet
(*Arbitrary Winds 2*)

————————

And because I had a hand in

creating the situation,

I am not stuck.

I can make choices and I can

choose again even if I can't see

the choices yet.

But if I look, honestly,

They will be revealed to me in time

and when **the time is**

the right time.

And today, I will ask myself whether IT'S JUST ALL TALK and

no action?

***

And when the signs do come
and the changes show themselves,
will I be ready to make them
and recognize it when I am presented
with new choices.

And will I be flexible and open enough
to know them when they get here or,
because I'm afraid, will I just let them
pass me by?

And will you be able to follow through
and take the actions right in front of you
that are really required

to take that step into the future
that you keep talking about
and saying you want?

Or will we just stay here,
where we are,
because it's easier than walking away
and taking the

risks.

Today, I will not beat myself up
if I CANNOT CONCENTRATE
MY NEGATIVE THOUGHTS
INTO THE POSITIVE

Sometimes it can seem like my thoughts are attacking me.

And sometimes it seems like it's impossible to change
your perspective or turn your head around
and turn your negative thoughts to the positive.

Because you've read every book that tells you
how much every thought you have is generative
which only makes it worse.

And when those times happen, it's hard
to believe that doing nothing to let it pass
might be the best course of action because,

in those moments, no matter how hard you try,
it feels like you're spinning your wheels and only

digging a hole.

But in those days, you can remember
that you've been in these moments before
and holes like these and even though they seem
like they never will when you're in them

they always pass.

em·brace - *[em-breys] verb*

to take or receive gladly or eagerly;

accept willingly: adopt, welcome: seize.

Today, I will embrace where I am

and how I feel

_____

for when I fight it,

sometimes it gives us more strength.

And when I embrace my good feelings they have the potential to skyrocket me into

another dimension.

Today, I will JUST LET IT BE WHAT HAPPENED

When we're in the middle, we can't see
and we attach ideas to ideas like why is this
happening to me
or am I being punished or what did I do to deserve
this?

Or we attach other ideas like I am so lucky
or I knew I could, I knew I could
or I won because I was so good and the world
really did give me the pay off and nice guys
really can finish first after all…

But what if we could just let what happened
 just be what happened
 without judging it good or bad…

And what if we could know that
every experience was just an experience
that was brought to us or that we ordered
to learn from,

that everything that happened to us
came for a purpose,
that this whatever it is
has come to us for a reason and not at random

so that you could outgrow the old lies that you
believed
and have been unknowingly perpetuating.

No matter where they

came from.

Today, I will let you PLEASE, SAVE YOUR NEGATIVITY

_____

Some people are flat out against you.

And some people are just worried about you

even though they're on your side.

But please keep your curses and doom

to yourself and save your worry

for me, about me and at me and your

bitter fruit that

I didn't order.

And stop jumping into my future.

I've already got enough to worry about without your

clever predicting.

Today, I will realize that

IT'S GOOD TO HAVE OLD FRIENDS

And that its important to have people who know you

even when you don't see each other all the time

or even for long periods of time.

Someone who knows the smooth criminal you are

and the pieces of you that get low and

understands because they know where you come from.

And the people who walked there with you before

and with whom you did it together.

And the ones who can call on each other

when you need to and when your real

chips are down.

Today, I will realize, sometimes
YOU JUST HAVE TO MAKE A DECISION

—————

And that point will come
stand or fall
when you'll have to choose.

To move forward or go back
and when you realize there's
no more time for sitting still.

That clock has run out
and that the old time is gone.
And you can try to please everybody else
or even just one someone else but that will
always come back to bite you.
Or you can try to make the decision

just for yourself but the truth is, there's no
real way to sort all of that out because
no matter how we want to sometimes,

I can't live in a vacuum.

And whether it's going back or
moving forwards or even trying to stay still
there really is no choice
because the days are going to
keep coming anyway and time doesn't

turn backwards.

Today, I will remember that it's easy to forget that EVERYBODY HAS PROBLEMS

and today I celebrate 18 years of sobriety.
It's easy to see that there is so much to be grateful for.

But it's also easy to say
"18 years for this."

But then you have to think of the high school cheerleader blonde who's surviving breast cancer

and the family who lost their son in Iraq, unresolved, or the Dad who has been out of work for two years feeling pieces of himself eroding away.

And I have the privilege to think about
the hundreds and hundreds of people
along the years and along the way
who brought a piece to my giant pie
and carried me when I couldn't move
and the fact that I should have been dead
many times over with no exaggeration
and it puts the difficulties of the present moment
in some perspective and I see that
in the same
thought moment,

I am almost the **luckiest** man

in the world.

Today, I will just let you HAVE
ALL THE MARBLES

———

Marbles are hard to buy these days.
They don't sell them everywhere like they used to.

Someone must be afraid that little children
will choke on them in a world that's become so

dangerous.

And did you really think that
if you ripped off the scab,
I'd try to bleed you to death?

And how much difference can a
little salt make for rubbing in
between friends
when so much resentment
has already gone under the bridge.

And when the moments of truth come,
who would have thought that you'd still be
trying to hold on to all the marbles,
not walking away or even sharing
the chalk if you won't come along

so I could at least walk away and go and draw

a new circle

and get a new set of better agates
to leave behind a history of

skinning knees.

Today, I will realize Things could get better or you could be getting free

———

So there really is no lose in this situation.

Although it's really hard to see through to it

with images of packed boxes and moving vans

and an emptying house that feel like heartbreak

running through your eyes.

Or to see that maybe there are chances
that things could get better when
everyday life has become so distant
but full of quiet taken sides at the same
time.

It can even be hard to just hope again.

And the questions still linger like

'Baby Baby, where did our love go?'
and 'How am I supposed to live without
you

after I been loving you so long?' and

'Did you think I'd crumble?
Did you think I'd lay down and

die?'

Today, I will make sure that my AFFAIRS ARE IN ORDER

And I will ask myself that
if today were my last day

if I were hit by a bus
or killed by a drunk driver walking on the street
would my affairs be in order?

And not the papers in folders
and drawers,

but who hadn't I loved and
what hadn't I said and who hadn't I loved

enough?

and what hadn't I let go...
like what anger had I let waste

too much of our time
and energy that I might be stuck with
on the way out or
that I'd let block me
from something better
since it just doesn't work that way?

And am I right with my "God"
whatever it is to me
that I'm carrying in me or am I just
walking by that part of myself in a crowd
because I don't want to go there.

And how have I treated and am I living
in alignment with myself

and I can ask myself
why haven't I taken care of these things

already, and what am I afraid of
that I'm letting block me?

Or is it just

easier?